LEGENDS OF THE END

PROPHECIES OF THE END TIMES, ANTICHRIST, APOCALYPSE, AND MESSIAH FROM EIGHT RELIGIOUS TRADITIONS

CHARLES UPTON

LEGENDS
OF THE END

*PROPHECIES OF THE END TIMES,
ANTICHRIST, APOCALYPSE,
& MESSIAH FROM EIGHT
RELIGIOUS TRADITIONS*

SOPHIA PERENNIS

HILLSDALE NY

First published in the USA
By Sophia Perennis
Series editor: James R. Wetmore
© copyright 2004

Series editor: James R. Wetmore

For information, address:
Sophia Perennis, P.O. Box 611
Hillsdale NY 12529
sophiaperennis.com

Printed in the United States of America

Library of Congress Cataloging-in-Publication Data

Upton, Charles, 1948–
Legends of the end: prophecies of the end times,
Antichrist, apocalypse, and Messiah from eight religious traditions.

p. cm.

ISBN 1 59731 025 5 (pbk : alk. paper)
ISBN 1 59731 021 2 (cloth : alk. paper)
1. Eschatology. I. Title
BL 500.U68 2004
202'.3—dc22   2004019283

CONTENTS

FACING APOCALYPSE

INTRODUCTION

AT THE BEGINNING of the third millennium, the human race is in the process of forgetting what it means to be human. We don't know who or what we are; we don't know what we are supposed to be doing here, in a cosmos rapidly becoming nothing to us but a screen for the projection of random and increasingly demonic fantasies. Human life is no longer felt to be valuable in the face of eternity simply because it is a creation of God, nor is it as easy as it once was for us to see the human enterprise as worth something because of our collective achievements or the historical momentum which produced them, since without a scale of values rooted in eternity, achievement cannot be measured, and without an eternal goal toward which time is necessarily tending (in the spiritual not the material sense, given that eternity cannot lie at the end of an accelerating linear momentum which is precisely a flight from all that is eternal), history is a road leading nowhere. The name we've given to this state of affairs is 'postmodernism'.

We all, somehow, know this. We feel it in our bones. But we can't encompass it; we can't define the scale of what we face or what we've lost, because we no longer possess the true scale of what we are. We assume the name postmodern, but it would be closer to the truth to say that we are *post-human*—not in essence, but in effect, since any concept of human nature adequate to the human essence has been discarded as *passé*.

Humanism is not enough to tell us what it is to be human. Science is even less capable of shouldering this burden, which is why it has mostly given up trying. Only religion, understood in its deepest sense, can ask this question and answer it. And only a thorough understanding of the social and psychic forces that hide the face of the Absolute and Infinite Reality we call 'God' can show us the true scale of what menaces the human form in these 'latter days', when the present cycle of biological and human time is drawing to a close.

If the name 'God' denotes the eternal truth of things, and the name 'Man' the central mirror of this Truth in terrestrial space and time, then the name of those forces of obscurity and denial which are opposed to 'Man', in their fully revealed and terminal form, is 'Antichrist'.

THE LATTER DAYS

It is common nowadays for many to imagine that the universe, in line with progressive and evolutionary ideas, must somehow be advancing spiritually. If we come to the conclusion that the spiritual evolution of the macrocosm is not possible, we may even wonder what is the worth or profit in material existence. What good is it? What is it for? For fear of becoming 'Gnostics' who deny the value of terrestrial life, we end by denying the *eternal* significance of this very life.

The problem with the concept that the universe evolves to higher levels of organization, which is basic to the doctrines of Teilhard de Chardin, Rudolf Steiner, and many other New Age teachers (as well as to the attempt within Judaism to apply Lurianic Kabbalah—and within Ismailism, the idea of a mass 'unveiling' of spiritual realities—to historical evolution) is the Second Law of Thermodynamics. This law states that, via entropy, the overall order of matter/energy in the universe is always decreasing, a decrease which is inseparable in principle from the expansion of the universe, starting at the Big Bang. At one point scientists posited the existence of large amounts of 'dark matter' which would allow the universe to contract again, via gravitation, after the momentum of the Big Bang is spent. As of this writing, however, scientific opinion is tending away from this hypothesis. So it would seem that the material universe must continue expanding, and its disorder increasing, forever.

This is strictly in line with traditional metaphysics. 'This whole world is on fire,' said the Buddha. 'All is perishing,' says the Koran, 'except His Face.' Creation, in the traditional view, is a successive 'stepping down' of a higher order of reality to lower ones. God, who in His Essence is totally beyond form, number, matter, energy, space and time, must—as Frithjof Schuon never tired of pointing out—'overflow' into these dimensions of existence because He is Infinite; no barrier exists in His Nature which would prevent the radiation of His superabundant Being.

Traditional eschatologies, by and large, are in line with the Second Law of Thermodynamics. In the place of progress—a myth no older than, perhaps, the 17th century, at least in its present form—they posit a spiritual, social and cultural 'entropy'. This is certainly true of Hinduism and classical Greco-Roman mythology, with their idea that a given cycle of manifestation emerges fully formed from the Creator in the form of a Golden Age, to be succeeded by a Silver Age, a Bronze Age, and finally by the present Iron Age, which ends in an eschatological cataclysm, a Purification Day, after which the Golden Age of the next cycle commences. This scheme is more or less accepted, through different mythological languages, by traditional Jews, Christians and Hindus, and even Lakota (Sioux) Indians, and other 'primal' peoples. (The Buddhists, though their doctrine of cycles tends to deny the possibility of an abrupt renewal, also accepts that the present era will end in cataclysm.) Those doctrines within traditional revealed religions which seem to speak of the spiritual progress of the manifest world itself, such as the concept in Lurianic Kabbalah of the *tikkun* or universal restoration, are either a mis-application of the lore of individual spiritual development to collective history, usually in line with 18th century Enlightenment ideas of progress and their Renaissance precursors; or of the doctrine that God continually creates and holds in existence this manifest world, and may therefore give an individual, religious dispensation or particular nation a special role in renewing the Divine Image for a given human time and place, within the larger context of overall spiritual degeneration; or of the eschatological return of all manifestation to God at the 'end of time'. Whatever is created must leave the House of the Creator in order to come into existence; whatever has emerged into cosmic manifestation has already begun to die.

Believers periodically predict the final (though temporary) triumph of evil in the latter days, the end of the world and the coming of the Messiah. Non-believers routinely scoff when such predictions seemingly fail to materialize. They will have the opportunity to continue scoffing until the world really does end, after which neither believers nor non-believers will, in worldly terms at least, have either the opportunity or the impulse to say 'I told you so.' At that ultimate moment of truth they will find themselves face-to-face with a Reality so profound, so rigorously demanding, that their opinions—right or wrong—along with all the psychological reasons they had for holding them, will dwindle into insignificance. Only their essential motive for holding to Truth or sinking into error will remain to them, as the sign of their eternal destiny before the face of God.

Non-believers say, 'some people in every generation have always thought they were living through the darkest times in history; all this whining about the degeneration of humanity in the "latter days" is nothing new.' And believers, at least traditional believers, agree with them. According to a *hadith* of the Prophet Muhammad (peace and blessings be upon him), 'no generation will come upon you that is not followed by a worse.' The course of history is not uniformly downward, in the traditional view—there are peaks and troughs, religious revivals, 'redresses', partial renewals of a given spiritual tradition leading to small and short-lived 'golden ages', heroic struggles of succeeding generations to cut their losses and re-stabilize society on lower levels, delirious renaissances based on the sudden impulse to squander the cultural and spiritual capital inherited from earlier ages—but the basic drift is always away from order and in the direction of chaos. The ability of the race to see, understand, draw its life from, and base its social and cultural forms on higher spiritual realities inevitably diminishes; as it speeds ever farther from the spiritual Sun, the light of Truth fades into the surrounding darkness; and the warmth of Life fades along with it. The final result of this inevitable process is the end of a particular world or world-age. This world may never end according to the time-table of those simple-minded people who take eschatological predictions literally, but it will have to end some time. And given that we presently have more ways at our disposal than ever before in human history of bringing this world to an end in concrete terms, through nuclear or chemical or biological warfare, or environmental degradation—or the deconstruction of the human form itself through a genetic engineering driven by blind economic forces, by the whims emotionally imbalanced or demonically inspired fools, and certainly by primal human fear and desire untempered by even the shadow of wisdom—a meditation on the End Times is timely, to say the least.

And, in sober fact, it is always timely. Every day a new generation passes into oblivion. It is always the worst of times: one day farther from the Garden of Eden, when the world, fresh from the Creator's hand, was young— and always the best of times: one day nearer to the inevitable Moment when contingency and illusion must crumble, and Absolute Reality dawn, definitively, upon this dying world, this moving image of Eternity.

THE ANTICHRIST

The spiritual degeneration of humanity cannot go on forever; it must reach a terminal point, beyond which the human form itself, at least in its earthly incarnation, could not survive. And in line with the principle of *corruptio optimi pessima*—'the corruption of the best is the worst'—the nadir of human spiritual receptivity must, according to the doctrine of many spiritual traditions, manifest not simply as the disappearance of spirituality, but as the satanic counterfeit of it. This is the origin of the myth of the Antichrist, which few in the West realize is as important in Islam as it is to Christianity, given that Muslims believe that the prophet Jesus will return to earth at the end of the age to give battle to that Adversary, and slay him in battle.

Just as the ego is the shadow of the Divine Self within us, so the Antichrist is the shadow of the Messiah, of the eschatological savior who represents the complete unveiling of the Divine Self at the end of this cycle. The ego will often reach a climax of despair, delusion and violence just when a spiritual breakthrough is imminent; in the same way the Antichrist will gather to himself all the social and psychic forces which have willed to resist God at the very moment the Face of the Absolute is about to dawn upon the world. The words of Meister Eckhart might well have been said of the Antichrist, as they were most certainly said of the human ego: 'The more he blasphemes, the more he praises God.'

THE MESSIAH

Throughout history, religions which look for a Messiah have always tended to concretize him. This or that Mahdi rises within Islam, only to be either co-opted or defeated. Sabbatai Zevi, the false Messiah, profoundly moves the whole Jewish world in the 17th century, and then converts, under threat of death by the Turkish Sultan, to Islam. And Christianity is certainly not without its false Christs and false prophets. So who is the real Messiah? How can we recognize him?

The real Messiah is eternally arriving in this world, eternally shattering its spatio-temporal dimensions, and eternally drawing his followers into the fellowship of His kingdom. To the degree that 'false' messiahs are receptive to this truth, they are actually in some sense partial messiahs, imperfect reflections of the Messiah himself. But to the degree that they identify with their messianic role on the level of the ego, thereby pandering to the collective ego of their followers—and they always do—they are antichrists. Humanity, sunk in materialism, cannot be awakened from 'the nightmare of history' without some form of historical hope. Yet this hope is always dashed. The revolution is co-opted. The renaissance fades. The spiritual renewal inevitably becomes food for the literalization of the doctrine and hardening of social and cultural lines. The Spirit is always giving life; the letter is always dragging that life into the tomb of contingency, into time and history. Those who, responding to messianic hope, pass from the turmoil of time to the vision of Eternity, have met the real Messiah. Those who fail to break their pact with time, either because they hope for something from fate and contingency, or foolishly believe they can manipulate them for their own ends, have fallen into the snare of the Antichrist.

So when will the real Messiah come? The answer is always twofold: he will come Now; he will come at the End. If we stand in the Now, we stand in wait for him; if we fail to occupy the Now, we will miss him when he comes. We have already missed him, times without number. But when Now and the End come together—the end of this ego, the end of this world—then we are standing in the presence of the Messiah.

History is always carrying us away from the day of the messianic advent, the door of the Now—and yet history must end some day; this endless departure must, in one mysterious moment, be changed into an arrival. What we receive in the secrecy of our hearts and what dawns on the 'horizons' of outer reality, must one day come together. In the words of the Koran, 'I will show them my signs on the horizons and in themselves, until they know that it is the Truth. Is this not enough for you, since I am over all things the Witness?'

THE PROPHECY OF RENÉ GUÉNON

My basic approach to the material presented in this book is that of traditional metaphysics, as presented by the writers of the Traditionalist School. For 'pure' metaphysics I have mostly followed Frithjof Schuon. For eschatology itself—the science of the 'last things'—I have relied on Martin Lings, particularly his book *The Eleventh Hour*, and even more so on the founder of the Traditionalists, René Guénon, whose prophetic masterpiece, *The Reign of Quantity and the Signs of the Times*, first published in 1945, grows more relevant with every passing year. But though it was the Traditionalists who pointed me in the direction of the scriptures of the world religions, the writings of the great sages and the legends of the primal peoples, I have not strictly limited myself in every case to their doctrines or perspectives, but have in many cases consulted the primary documents themselves. To paraphrase Blake, I have looked through their eyes, not with them.

In *The Reign of Quantity*, Guénon saw history in terms of the Hindu concept of the *manvantara*, the cycle of manifestation composed of Golden, Silver, Bronze, and Iron ages. He saw this cycle as an inevitable descent from the pole of Essence, or *forma*— the Hindu *Purusha*—toward the pole of Substance, or *materia*—the Hindu *Prakriti*. Essence is qualitative, while actually lying above quality. Substance is quantitative, while in reality situated below quantity.

As the cycle progresses, or rather descends, the very nature of time and space changes. In earlier ages, space dominates; the forms of things are more important, more real, than the changes they undergo; time is 'relatively eternal'. As the cycle moves on, however, time begins to take over, melting down space and the forms within it until everything is an accelerating flow of change.

Maybe we can better understand what Guénon was talking about if we notice that when we are a state of deep calm, space is more real than time; when we are agitated, time becomes more real than space. And it shouldn't be too hard to see how faster modes of travel, and especially the electronic media, which disturb and agitate consciousness, also annihilate space; cyberspace, in particular, is the annihilation of all spacial dimension. In these latter days, nothing has a stable form. Everything moves faster and faster, until all form—including the Human Form itself—becomes a shapeless blur.

But this constant acceleration of time can't go on forever. At one point it will have to stop. 'Time the devourer,' quotes Guénon, 'ends by devouring itself.' At the end of time, time will instantaneously be changed into space again. This ultimate, timeless point is simultaneously the end of this cycle of manifestation and the beginning of the 'next'.

But before this ultimate transformation, in the latter days of the present cycle, certain final developments must take place. Since quantity has particularly to do with matter, the 'reign of quantity' must also be the reign of materialism—and where materialistic ideas dominate, the very cosmic environment becomes in a sense more material. The 'age of miracles' ceases; the world becomes less permeable to the influences of higher planes of reality; the very belief in such planes, as well as in an eternal and transcendent God, becomes harder to maintain.

The very heaviness of materialism, however, ultimately results in a sort of 'brittleness'. The cosmic environment, having lost much of the flexibility which allowed it to be moved by the Divine Spirit, begins to crack, like an old tree that can no longer bend to the wind, and ends by being uprooted in the storm. But these cracks in the cosmic environment, in the 'Great Wall' separating the material world from the realm of subtle energies, first happen in the 'downward' rather than the 'upward' direction, letting in a flood of 'infrapsychic' forces, either neutral or actively demonic. In the general 'volatilization' of the sense-world produced by the electronic media and our 'information culture', perhaps also by the prevalence of electromagnetic pollution and the release of nuclear energy; by the contemporary interest in psychedelic drugs, magic and psychic powers; and most obviously by what we've come to call the 'UFO phenomenon' which has had an incalculable effect upon our common view of reality, we can see the direct effects of these forces on the quality of our consciousness, the structure of our society, our cultural forms and our economic priorities.

Nor do these infra-psychic forces operate alone. Cultural trends develop around the infra-psychic *zeitgeist*, and within the context of these trends, organized groups grow up in response to the forces which have brought them into being. In some cases these groups are simply made up of people who espouse the modernist or postmodernist myths determined by the 'spirit of the times'. Other groups, however, will openly worship the forces which have inspired them, not understanding that they have in fact taken a stand against the perennial wisdom, the metaphysical truths of the ages. These Guénon terms 'anti-traditional' or 'pseudo-initiatic'. Most New Age organizations would fall under this definition. And lastly, there are other groups whose goal is to deliberately undermine revealed religion and traditional metaphysics, so as to bring in the reign of the Antichrist; these, in Guénon's terms, are the agents of 'counter-tradition' and the 'counter-initiation'; they are 'Satan's contemplatives', whose role is to subvert, not simply exoteric religion, but esoteric spirituality as well.

However depressing this may sound, the truth is that such developments are entirely lawful, given the lateness of the hour. The lowest possibilities of manifestation must also have their day in the course of the cycle; fortunately, since they are inherently unstable, being based not upon Truth but solely upon power, that day will be short. 'There needs be evil,' said Jesus, 'but woe to him through whom evil comes.' And there are certain spiritual possibilities of the highest order which could never be realized except in the face of this most demonic of challenges to the integrity of the human spirit.

The times we live in have been called 'postmodern'. What exactly does this mean? What could possibly come after being 'up to date'? And if something really might come after, how could we possibly be contemporary with it? Does 'postmodern' mean 'after history'? Could it, perhaps, have something to do with the 'end of time'?

Here is postmodernism in a nutshell:

(1) There is no objective truth, therefore, (2) reality is not perceived but rather constructed, by inherent patterns of perception, or by history, or by society and language, or by the individual, thus (3) all attempts to create comprehensive world-views that transcend history, or society, or even (ultimately) the individual are oppressive, therefore (4) all such arbitrarily constructed worldviews should be deconstructed in order to celebrate diversity and preserve the rights of marginalized minority constructions of reality.

But without the liberating and stabilizing presence of objective reality outside the 'me', [a reality] where all subjective standpoints converge, everything is ego—and the ego is defined not by truth but by power. This ego, however, having no intrinsic reality, is in fact the weakest of all imaginable pseudo-realities. As such, its solipsism is destined to be devoured by a larger solipsism, a greater unreality, a more powerful weakness—by the regime of those who, in the name of power, have most completely emptied

themselves of reality, in the service of that greatest unreality, that most powerful weakness of all—the Antichrist. In Guénon's words,

The Antichrist must . . . be as near as it is possible to be to 'disintegration', so that one could say that his individuality, while it is developed in a monstrous fashion, is nevertheless at the same time almost annihilated, thus realizing the inverse of the effacement of the 'ego' before the 'Self', or in other words, realizing confusion in 'chaos' as against fusion in principial Unity. . . .[1]

1. *The Reign of Quantity and the Signs of the Times*, (Hillsdale, NY: Sophia Perennis, 2004), p273.

Postmodernism, in its understandable attempt to avoid totalitarian ideologies, it is storing up in the collective unconscious, through its own "totalitarian relativism," a deep desire for the lost Unity which was once provided by religion, metaphysics and the intellectual intuition of God. When our exhaustion with chaos and relativism reaches the breaking-point—which will also be the point when our ability to recognize true, objective, metaphysical Unity is most deeply eroded—then our unconscious desire for that Unity will explosively emerge. And the one who can best fulfill this desire, on a global level—no matter how unrealistic his promises are, since our collective sense of reality will then be at its lowest ebb—will step into the role of Antichrist.

GLOBALISM AND ANTICHRIST

Globalism and One World Government, in my opinion, are not the system of Antichrist, though they are among the factors which will make that regime possible.

I believe that the system of Antichrist will emerge—is in fact emerging—out of the conflict between the New World Order and the spectrum of militant reactions against it.

In Jesus' time, the One World Government was the Roman Empire. The Zealots were the anti-Roman revolutionaries and/or militias. Jesus was careful not to be drawn into making statements which would compromise the Zealot cause and make him appear as a Roman collaborator. But he also related to Roman military officers, and toadies of Rome like the Jewish tax collectors, in ways that scandalized many Jewish nationalist patriots. He emerged from the common people oppressed both by Rome and by the colonial Jewish ruling classes who did Rome's dirty work, and he denounced those sectors of the ruling class—the Scribes, Pharisees, Sadducees and Herodians—who made common cause with the Empire, while speaking no word against the Zealots and Essenes, who did not. But he did not identify with the violent 'vanguard' who acted in the people's name. So we can say that if Christ worked to avoid being identified either with the Roman Empire or with its militant opponents, by the same token we should be careful not to strictly identify Antichrist either with One World Government or with anti-globalist terrorism. Together they will provide the milieu out of which he will emerge; but just as Christ avoided being claimed by either party because it was his mission to redeem not the Jews alone but all humanity, so Antichrist will 'play both sides against the middle' in the latter days to build his power over all aspects of the human soul. Antichrist is not primarily the enemy of democracy or national autonomy, in other words, but of Humanity itself, considered as made in the image and likeness of God. In its deepest essence, the battle between Christ and Antichrist is not between freedom and tyranny (though where true freedom is, the Antichrist cannot come), nor between traditional religious bodies and secular society (though the field of this conflict may, at least in some cases, be closer to the real war), but that between the sacred presence of God in the human heart, and the sacrilegious violation of that presence: 'When ye therefore shall see the Abomination of Desolation, spoken of by Daniel the prophet, stand in the holy place (whoso readeth, let him understand), then let them which be in Judea flee into the mountains' (Matt. 24:15–16).

Globalism is in the process of destroying all traditional and national cultures, undermining and compromising all traditional religious forms. But to simply oppose all planning and action on a global scale is also problematic. The ironic truth is that given globalism, we need globalism. If business is international, unions must be international too, or wages might eventually be driven below the subsistence level everywhere. If epidemics are global, public health efforts must cross national boundaries. If pollution is global, efforts to limit it must be global. If crime is global, the police must be also. If 'emerging' nations and terrorist gangs develop weapons of mass destruction, efforts must be made to limit their spread. We have no choice but to try and manage the earth on a planetary level. But the struggle to accomplish this is itself producing ambiguous results. If the powers that be can use environmentalism, public health efforts, armed peacemaking and the war against international crime, terrorism and the drug trade to further consolidate their power, they will. Or rather, they are. Anyone who opposes the effort to save the environment or cut into the international drug trade or limit the possibility of nuclear terrorism is working against the best interests of humanity and the earth. But anyone who identifies with these efforts or places his or her hopes in them is deluded. The earth cannot be managed on a planetary level because the forces of globalism which aspire to do the managing—global business and finance in other words, followed and not led by the trend toward political unification—are the same forces which are creating these problems in the first place. The global spread of industry and exploitation of resources—originated and presently driven, despite the communist interlude, by trans-national capitalism—are the origin of environmental degradation. By destroying traditional subsistence economies and proletarianizing labor—helped greatly in this by the brutal collectivization of agriculture, at the expense of tens of millions of lives, in communist Russia and China—by exploiting cheap labor and threatening national and religious cultural identities, the forces of global capitalism have themselves created the global underground trade in drugs, weapons, endangered animal species, slaves... all monuments to the entrepreneurial spirit. Only a One World Government could possibly limit the destructive power of these international economic forces. But when and if such a government emerges, even though it may have some mitigating influence on global disasters, it will be the agent of these forces, not their adversary.

Politics is the art of the ephemeral. Whatever of human value is gained through political action is temporary, ambiguous and corruptible. This is the nature of time and history—of matter itself. Action for social justice, action to save the environment are laudable. Every person who can avoid being crushed by circumstances without becoming an exploiter and oppressor of others is a blessing to the race. Every species which can be saved from extinction remains as an incomparable mirror of one unique aspect of the Divine nature, and may (or may not) add to the biodiversity available in the next cycle of terrestrial manifestation, since we can't absolutely know whether or not the end of this *aeon* must entail the total destruction of all life on earth, or even all human life; all we know is that it will be the end for 'us'.

But the battle against Antichrist is on a different level. Though for some it may include a political expression, it is essentially spiritual. 'My kingdom is not of this world.' It is a struggle to save, not the world, but the human soul—starting, and finishing if necessary, with one's own.

COMPARATIVE
ESCHATOLOGY

ESCHATOLOGY is the science of four 'last things': individual death; individual destiny in the afterlife; the end of this world or cycle of manifestation; the renewal of life and existence after that end. This essay deals with the latter two—with apocalypse, the re-absorption of forms by their celestial archetypes, and the re-manifestation of those forms in the 'Golden Age' of the cycle to come. In this chapter I compare the eschatological lore of eight traditions: Zoroastrianism, Hinduism, Buddhism, Judaism, Christianity, Islam, the Hopi, and the Lakota. When viewed synoptically, the prophecies of these eight traditions appear as rays, or facets, of a single Form.

According to a hadith of the Prophet Muhammad collected by Muslim, as paraphrased by William Chittick,

> God will appear at the resurrection in a multitude of forms, but His creatures will deny Him until He appears in a form that corresponds to their own belief. It is only the perfect men, whose hearts encompass all the Divine Names in perfect equilibrium, who will recognize God in whatever form He displays.

SAOSHYANT VS. ANGRA MAINYU
ZOROASTRIAN ESCHATOLOGY

Prophecies of the 'end times' from many traditions predict a degeneration of spirituality, civilization, and the environment leading to an apocalyptic conflict. But it seems likely that Zarathustra (Zoroaster) was the first to sum up all the forces opposed to religion and human life in a single figure: Angra Mainyu (later called Ahriman). Many ancient gods had their dark antagonists; Set, for example, was the brother and enemy of the Egyptian Osiris. But most of these antagonisms were seen in terms of the yearly cycle of the seasons, or the heroic exploits of a world-sustaining savior, like the demon-subduing Krishna. Zarathustra, however, conceived of the struggle of light against darkness in terms of the entire cycle of manifestation, envisioning a definitive victory of the forces of light at the end of time, during the apocalyptic event called in ancient Persian *Frashegird*. Thus many scholars see Zoroastrianism as the original ancestor of Judeo-Christian eschatology, and Angra Mainyu as the prototype of both Satan and the Antichrist. The coming eschatological savior, Saoshyant, is the Zoroastrian equivalent of the Hindu Kalki Avatara, the Jewish Messiah, the Christ of the second coming, the Muslim Mahdi, and similar in many ways to the future Buddha, Maitreya.

The central theophany in Zoroastrianism is fire, which is also the prime agent of the Last Judgement. In the account of Frashegird from the *Bundahish*, a great meteor will strike the earth [cf. Rev. 8:10–11; 9:1ff.] and kindle the eschatological fire. Rivers of molten metal will flow. To the righteous they will seem like warm milk; to the unrighteous, like molten metal. The wise experience the flame of Ahura Mazda ('Lord of Wisdom') as light—in other words, enlightenment; the deceitful, as punishing fire. According to the Zoroastrian scriptures called the *Yashts*, some of which are believed to go back to c.2000 BC,

> in order that the dead shall rise up, that Living One, the Indestructible, shall come, the world be made wonderful at his wish.... When Astvaterets [Saoshyant] comes out from Lake Kansaoya, messenger of Mazda Ahura, son of Vispatauvairi [his virgin mother], brandishing the victorious weapon ... then he will drive the Drug ['Deception', an epithet of Angra Mainyu] from the world of Asha [Divine Law]. He will gaze with wisdom, he will behold all creation ... he will gaze with eyes of sacrifice on the whole material world, and heedfully will he make the whole material world undying.... An[g]ra Mainyu of evil works will flee, bereft of power.[2]

2. *Yasht* 19.

One wonders if the Pahlevi *drug* or *druj* is related to the Syriac word *daggal* which also denotes 'deception', and from which *dajjal,* the Arabic name for Antichrist, is derived.

To prophesy that Saoshyant will immortalize the material world through *heedfulness,* and by *gazing on it with wisdom* and *with eyes of sacrifice* is to say that the world will transformed, via the sacrifice of the human ego, from a literal material object into a theophany, a vision of the eternal Names of God; it will once again be seen as Adam saw it in Eden. In Blake's words, from *The Marriage of Heaven and Hell,*

> The ancient tradition that the world will be consumed in fire at the end of six thousand years is true. . . . For the cherub with his flaming sword is hereby commanded to leave his guard at the tree of life, and when he does, the whole creation will be consumed, and appear infinite and holy, whereas now it appears finite & corrupt. This will come to pass by an improvement of sensual enjoyment.

The function of Man is to act as God's eye on the created world, to unite it with its Archetype through divine contemplation, and only secondarily to work, in line with this contemplative vision, with natural forces and conditions. As human consciousness is purified in the spiritual and eschatological fire, the world will lose its literalistic 'materiality' (which, as pure negation, is not itself capable of being saved) and become what it always was, an immortal paradise. This apocalyptic restoration of the natural world is very close to the idea of the redemption of the cosmos in Eastern Orthodox Christianity, where the sacrament of the Eucharist, by which Christ's Incarnation and Redemption are propagated throughout space and time, is sometimes identified with the transfiguration of the universe. In the words of Orthodox theologian Olivier Clement,

> The world was created as an act of celebration, so that it might share in grace and become Eucharist through the offerings of human beings. And that is precisely what Christ, the last Adam, has accomplished. By his death and resurrection he has brought

glory to the universe. It is this transfigured creation that is offered to us in the Eucharist. . . .[3]

According to most scholars, Zarathustra lived around 660 BC. Yet linguistic evidence indicates that the 17 *Gathas*, those parts of the Zoroastrian scriptures (the *Avesta*) which were composed directly by him, may be as much as 4,000 years old. Whether another Zarathustra actually lived in 2000 BC, or whether the historical Zarathustra acted as the prophetic renewer of an older tradition, composing his *Gathas* in an archaic sacerdotal language, the Zoroastrian religion is of great antiquity; even if it was not the direct ancestor of the Abrahamic faiths, it profoundly influence all three of them. We must always remember, however, that no authentic religious tradition is patched together out of historical influences. If one tradition contributes material to another, it is only because they share the same essential Truth — and because the host tradition, in terms of the place and time in which it is destined to appear, is the privileged receptacle of that Truth.

MESSIAH:

JEWISH ESCHATOLOGY

This section is largely based on Gershom Scholem's
The Messianic Idea in Judaism,

The shadowy figure of the Messiah appears in many places throughout Jewish scripture: in the major and minor prophets; in the *Psalms*; in *Genesis*; also in many apocryphal books such as *Fourth Ezra*, *First* and *Second Enoch*, the *Baruch* apocalypses and the *Testament of the Twelve Patriarchs*. Many conceptions of his nature coalesce: he will be a king of the house of David; a priest of the line of Levi, or Aaron; he will vanquish Israel's enemies and establish a kingdom of peace. As a king, he is like David come back; as a renewer of the law, he is like Moses. The concept of the 'suffering servant'

---

3. *The Roots of Christian Mysticism*, p110.

from Isaiah 53, who through his death brings redemption to others, also became attached to the figure of the Messiah. According to Scholem, pp50–51,

> Only after the Bible did . . . varying conceptions as that of an ideal state of the world, of a catastrophic collapse of history, of the restoration of the Davidic kingdom, and of the 'Suffering Servant' merge with the prophetic view of the 'Day of the Lord' and a 'Last Judgement.

Messianic Judaism tends to downplay individual redemption in favor of the redemption of the nation, and ultimately the world. The Messianic Age is viewed as a total renovation, or restoration, of earthly life as God meant it to be. (Scholem sees the tendency of Christianity to emphasize individual redemption, in this world or the world to come, as one of the places where it diverges from the Jewish idea. Yet Jesus, in his crucifixion, rejected individual salvation in his own case, taking upon himself the sins of the nation and the race, just as the Zaddik in Hasidism may suffer personally to gather the scattered 'sparks' of the Divine Immanence, the *Shekinah*.)

Jewish Messianism is traditionally revolutionary and catastrophic. Through the Messianic breakthrough may be either gradual or instantaneous, it is not a product of historical development. Rather, the Light of God breaks through from a transcendent Source, destroys history and totally transforms it. Scholem characterizes the atmosphere preceding the coming of the Messiah as a time of

> world wars and revolutions . . . epidemics, famine, and economic catastrophe . . . apostasy and the desecration of God's name . . . , the upsetting of all moral order to the point of dissolving the laws of nature (p12).

According to the *Mishnah*,

> In the footsteps of the Messiah presumption will increase and respect disappear. The empire will turn to heresy and there will be no moral reproof. The house of assembly will become a brothel galilee will be laid waste, and the people of the frontiers

will wander from city to city and none will pity them. The
wisdom of the scribes will become odious and those who shun
sin will be despised; truth will nowhere be found. Boys will
shame old men and old men will show deference to boys. 'The
son reviles the father, the daughter rises up against the mother'
(Micah 7:6). The face of the generation is like the face of a dog.
On whom shall we then rely? Our father in heaven.

Moses Maimonides (who rejects the miraculous and apocalyptic
conception of the Messiah, the resurrection of the dead, etc.) has
this to say about his advent:

> The Messiah will arise and restore the kingdom of David to its
> former might. He will rebuild the sanctuary and gather the
> dispersed of Israel. All the laws will be reinstituted in his days as
> of old. Sacrifices will be offered and Sabbatical and Jubilee years
> will be observed exactly in accordance with the commandments
> of the Torah. But whoever does not believe in him or does not
> await his coming denies not only the rest of the prophets, but
> also the Torah and our teacher Moses.

Maimonides repeats the tradition that the war between Gog and
Magog and the return of the prophet Elijah will take place before
the Messiah's coming, maintaining however that 'no one knows
how they will come about until they actually happen.'

The messianic *tikkun* or restoration as presented in the kabbal-
ism of Isaac Luria is utopian and post-millennialist rather than
apocalyptic; it will happen when, through human spiritual labor, all
the scattered sparks of the Shekinah are gathered together again and
the 'vessels' restored, which burst at the moment of the creation
because they could not withstand the outpouring of God's power.
Yet it gave rise to the basically pre-millennialist messianic movement of Sabbetai Zevi, which ended in apparent disaster when the
'false Messiah' converted to Islam under threat by the Sultan of Tur-
key, whom he had attempted to convert to his brand of Judaism, in
1666. Sabbatianism, though not politically militant, was a true mass
movement. Its shameful and shocking failure, according to
Scholem, set the stage for the post-millennialist and spiritualizing

movement of Hasidism under Israel Baal Shem Tov, which re-interpreted messianism, at least initially, in radically interior terms.

According to traditional Judaism, the Jews are cautioned not to 'press for the End', since the coming of the Messiah is in the hands of God alone. Yet the fervent belief in that coming, not surprisingly, sometimes resulted in religious and political activism based on chiliastic ideas, which routinely ended in disaster. And, partly in response to the failure of such Messianic utopianism, there developed within the stream of the Kabbalah another more introverted way of 'pressing for the End'. It was believed that the great Kabbalist or Zaddik has the power to bring the Messiah through inner spiritual struggle, theurgy, or magic. He can descend into the realm of darkness, the world of the *kelipot*, the 'shells' or 'husks' (the root principles of materialism?), which he has the power to 'sweeten', thereby transmuting the wrath of God, gathering the scattered sparks of the Shekinah and reuniting them with the Creator. In so doing, he prepares the way for the Messiah. The great spiritual master, in other words, has the power to harrow Hell, like Christ did; *but this work is forbidden*. A legend is told of a great kabbalistic magician who captured Sammael, the Devil, and could therefore have brought about the redemption of Israel—if only he had not been seduced by his captive. (That the magical attempt to overcome evil on the macrocosmic level is forbidden to the Zaddik or Kabbalist is paralleled by the legend that Jesus was one of 30 saints of his time who had the power to bring back the dead; they were forbidden to do this, but Jesus broke the rules!)

According to some authorities, when the Messiah comes he will bring a new Torah; in the Biblical account, however, he will simply reveal the Torah in its fullness. The *Talmud* says that in the Messianic age the Torah will either be obeyed more strictly and perfectly than is possible now, or mostly abrogated. (According to the extremist and antinomian followers of Sabbetai Zevi, it will be entirely abrogated; whatever is now prohibited, in the Messianic age will be allowed, if not required.) A stricter and more complete Torah and a largely or totally abrogated one appear as extreme opposites. But could there be, by any chance, a hidden identity between them?

The *Zohar*, the central classic of kabbalistic literature attributed to Moses Cordovero, may provide the answer. According to the more recent parts of the *Zohar*, and their exegesis by the Sabbetians, there are two Torahs: the Torah of the Tree of Life and the Torah of the Tree of Knowledge of Good and Evil. The Torah of the Tree of Life is the Law as it was in Paradise before Adam sinned, the pure expression of God's creative power and wisdom, with no admixture of privation or evil. The Torah of the Tree of Knowledge is the Torah as we know it now in this fallen world.

Since both trees, according to the tradition, sprout from the same root, it could be said that the Tree of the Knowledge is an edited version, or darkened vision, of the Tree of Life. The first set of the tablets of the Law brought by Moses from Sinai, which he destroyed when he saw the people worshipping the Golden Calf, held the Torah of the Tree of Life. The second set contained the Torah of the Tree of the Knowledge of Good and Evil.

The meaning of this tradition is fairly clear: this fallen world is Paradise as seen through the veils of the ego. As long as the consequences of Adam's sin have not been suffered through and expiated under the influence of God's grace, the ego is still in force, the world still effectively (if not essentially) fallen. And the ego of this fallen world cannot withstand, or understand, the Torah of the Tree of Life, where everything is lawful because everything is a manifestation or an act of God. It interprets the primal power and innocence of God's Self-manifestation not as a fullness of Divine Life into which no evil can come, but as a Divine validation of chaos, and thus a as license to harm oneself and others. What on a higher level of interpretation is Paradise (the summit of Sinai being the symbol of this higher level), on a lower one is a worship of the unredeemed passions, the Golden Calf—in Sufi terms, the 'commanding self'. Moses brought the higher Law by which man is reunited to his Creator; the people could only see this as a reinstitution of Paganism. (In the same way, St Paul's doctrine that Christians were no longer under 'the curse of the law' led in some instances to libertinism, as in the excesses of the *agape* feasts railed against in the epistle of *Jude*.) Therefore a second, edited version of the Torah, tailored to this fallen order of perception, had to be substituted, a Torah based on commands and prohibitions, on 'the Knowledge of Good and Evil'. (The Torah of the Tree of Life is strictly analogous to the Islamic *Rahman*, God's universal and all-creating mercy, and to Ibn al-'Arabi's concept of the Divine Will, which is the cause of everything that actually occurs, thus in a sense making everything lawful — to God, that is. And the Torah of the Tree of the Knowledge of Good and Evil corresponds to the Islamic *Rahim*, God's particular and saving mercy, and to Ibn al-'Arabi's Divine Wish, the basis of the Muslim *shari'at* which is incumbent on all believers — because human beings are not God. The Torah of the Tree of Knowledge would also correspond to the figure of Moses in the Koran, and the Torah of the Tree of Life to the immortal prophet Khidr, whom the Sufis identify with the unnamed master, shocking and incomprehensible in his actions, encountered by Moses in the Koran, Surah of *The Cave*.)

In the Messianic age, the Torah of the Tree of Knowledge is replaced by the Torah of the Tree of Life. In a sense this is a 'new' Torah — though in reality it is simply the old one, understood now in its fullness. This Torah is more strictly and perfectly obeyed than was possible in the past because now that the fullness of God's Life has been unveiled to all men, it is virtually impossible to disobey it. Torah has risen from the level of the will, which can choose to obey or disobey, and come to rest on the level of the Intellect, where all is Truth. Truth commands obedience not through specific commands and prohibitions, but simply by being what It is. Truth is obeyed not through the struggle to remain faithful to behavioral norms, but simply by being recognized. And where commands and prohibitions are transcended, the Law is abrogated — not through being broken, however, but through being perfectly fulfilled. (In the words of Jesus, 'I come not to destroy the Law, but to fulfill it.') In Taoist terms, the Tao, the Way—perfectly analogous, on one level, to the Torah of the Tree of Life—is followed by means of *wu wei*, 'not doing', or 'acting without acting'. In *wu wei*, the dichotomy between assuming active responsibility and simply letting things take their course is entirely transcended; this is how it will be in the Messianic age.

According to the Aggadah, the Messiah was born on the day the second Temple was destroyed, and is now in occultation, like the

Shiïte Twelfth Imam. In 2nd century legend, well before the estab-
lishment of the Roman papacy, he is pictured as residing secretly in
Rome. It is as if the Jews said to the Romans, 'You destroy our Temple? Very well: the very spirit and principle of our Temple will then
become the hidden ruler of your own Empire.' In later years this
legend gave Jews a traditional basis for seeing the Pope as a counterfeit or anti-messiah, a kind of usurper of the secret messianic rule.
The *Tractate Sanhedrin* of the Talmud says that 'The Son of David
will not come until the kingdom is subverted to heresy.' It is difficult
not to see in this tradition a prediction that the tremendous genius
of the Jewish people will be diverted in psychic and materialistic
directions—as represented by Freud and Marx, for example, as well
as by the present secularism of the State of Israel.

Sometimes the figure of the Messiah is doubled: there will be a
Messiah son of Joseph as well as a Messiah son of David. The Messiah son of Joseph—although he is not, as Scholem points out, to be
identified with the 'suffering servant of Isaiah—perishes in the
eschatological combat, defeated by Antichrist. After this the Messiah son of David comes, kills the Antichrist, and establishes the
Kingdom. (The figure of Antichrist in Judaism, though based in
part on the Gog of *Ezekiel* and the Fourth Beast in *Daniel*, only
makes his fully developed appearance in the Jewish apocrypha.)
This tradition is closely paralleled by the Shiïte Muslim story that
when the Mahdi comes he will be defeated and killed by the Antichrist, after which the Antichrist himself will be slain by the prophet
Jesus.

According to the commentary on *Habakkuk* in the *Dead Sea
Scrolls*, the priestly Messiah of the End of Days, like Adam, will
encompass past present and future, and so be able to interpret the
visions of the ancient prophets regarding the total course of the history of Israel. Like the Kalki Avatara, and the Word of God in the
Christian *Apocalypse*, he is 'the beginning and the end'.

In the 10th chapter of the *Tractate Sanhedrin* from the Talmud, it
is said that 'The Son of David will come only in a generation wholly
guilty or a generation wholly innocent.' The messianic breakthrough into a totally corrupt world is necessarily pre-millennialist,
since the Messiah must then establish righteousness by means of a

revolutionary and apocalyptic cataclysm, just as his appearance in an already-purified world must be post-millennialist. Isaac Luria's messianic *tikkun*, for example, is post-millennialist; in Lurianic Kabbalah, the Messiah comes when we have sufficiently purified ourselves through our own actions; he is an automatic reflection of this purity. On the other hand, the Messianic movements of Bar Kochba and Sabbatai Zevi, the one political and military, the other mystical and spiritual, were necessarily pre-millennialist. These conceptions, like those of the abrogation vs. the perfect observance of the Torah, would seem to be totally opposed. Once again, however, it is the *Zohar* which points out, though in a veiled way, their hidden identity.

Following the Aggadah, the *Zohar* sees the Messianic breakthrough as gradual, though not thereby as the product of a historical development. The coming of the Messiah is not a human achievement, but a divine miracle. According to the *Zohar*, the gentiles (called 'Esau' or 'Edom') received their illumination at a single stroke, after which they slowly began to lose it. Israel, on the other hand, received its illumination gradually. As the loss of strength and illumination among the gentiles continues, Israel will slowly grow in power and knowledge, to the point where they will be able to overcome them and destroy them. After this the divine light will grow in Israel to the point where all things will be restored. The separation between creature and Creator will be transcended. The world will return to the state of Eden, and every man and woman will behold the Shekinah 'eye to eye'.

My exegesis of this doctrine is as follows: The gentiles or 'Esau' are the outer world of creation; they are history itself. 'Israel', on the other hand, is the inner world of the soul. According to Hindu and Greco-Roman doctrine, the cosmic cycle of manifestation begins with a God-given Golden Age, and then degenerates; the 'nations' receive their illumination all at once, then progressively lose it.

This 'historical entropy' is related to the net entropy of all physical processes. The very existence of a sensual world 'outside' the perceiving subject is in fact an expression of this entropy: if the Sun and the stars were not burning themselves away, we would not see anything; if matter were not crumbling, vaporizing, eroding and dissolving, we would not hear or smell or feel or taste anything. Matter *is* entropy. The expanding universe represents the dissipation inherent in everything material, as well as the ultimate fate of all those to whom matter is the central reality.

In the inner dimension of the soul, however, the opposite motion takes place. To the degree that one's sense of reality is withdrawn from the sensual world and placed on the ascending ladder of Being which is 'inner' in relation to that world, the pull of the senses and the heavy literalism of historical reality lose force, till the contemplation of spiritual realities conquers and overcomes the oppressive force of material contingencies; this is the return from 'captivity' and 'exile' and the entry into 'the Promised Land'. First we rise to an understanding of the sensual, material world as a subjective, psychic experience; secondly, the ultimate spiritual Witness of this psychic experience of the material world is progressively unveiled. As the outer world is always expanding and dissipating, so the inner world, to the degree that we place our attention upon it, is always being 'recollected', always coming to a point. (In Sufi terms, the outer world is the realm of *tafraqa*, dispersion, and the inner one the realm of *jam'*, gathering or concentration.) This simultaneous and double motion can be represented by two superimposed triangles, where the apex of the lower triangle (the manifestation of YHVH by means of creation) is the central point of the base of the upper triangle (the return to YHVH through spiritual contemplation), and vice versa. This diagram is a form of the Shield or Star of David (the Seal of Solomon), which is one emblem of the Adam Kadmon (another being the kabbalistic Tree of Life of the ten *sephiroth*) who in the eschatological dimension is the Messiah as well: the 'Human Form Divine', created in the 'image and likeness of God', being the secret form of YHVH, which transcends and thereby encompasses both His creation of the cosmos and the universal *tikkun* of the cosmos to its root in Him.

When the 'generation' of the outer world is wholly guilty and corrupt—when it is completely dead to us, since we have died to it—then the 'generation' of the inner world will be wholly innocent, since it knows only God, Who is 'of too pure eyes to behold iniquity.' It is precisely in this sense that the Messiah will come in a

'generation' which is totally innocent in one sense and totally corrupt in another.

But the Messiah, like Adam, does not exclusively represent the
triumph of inner recollection over outer manifestation, material
and historical, but encompasses both dimensions. The Jewish hope
for a restored terrestrial kingdom is not simply abandoned or
superseded therefore, but rather totally transformed. As in the
Christian *Apocalypse*, the messianic kingdom—the New Jerusalem,
bride of the Messiah—represents both a new heaven and a new
earth.

According to the *Zohar*, the Messiah will not come until the tears
of Esau are exhausted. This is the same story told in a different way.
Jacob is 'Israel', the name he received after his struggle with the
angel at Peniel, in the course of which he overcame the 'descending'
current of manifestation and entered the 'ascending' current of
tikkun, these being the two directions in which the angels moved in
his dream of the Ladder, which is a type of the kabbalistic Tree of
Life. In the context of this world, he came out of the struggle lame;
in the context of the next world, he won the blessing of God. Jacob's
brother Esau, then, represents the attachment to the descending
current of creation—so fresh and childlike in Eden—which ultimately leads to dissipation in the materialistic vision of things that
will always sell its invisible birthright, its share in the world to
come, for 'a mess of pottage', the visible material goods of this
world. (That Jacob could only get the patriarchal blessing from his
blind father Isaac through deceit represents the fact that the path of
tikkun is inner and esoteric. That one aspect of this deceit required
Jacob to dress in an animal skin so that Isaac would believe he was
blessing his hairy son Esau represents the transfiguration of the
materialistic or animalistic lower nature of man on the Path of its
return to the Creator.) The color of Esau, Isaac's first-born, and also
of the pottage for which he sold his birthright, is red. Red symbolizes creation, primal life-energy; Esau shares this color-symbolism
with Adam, the first-created man, whose name means 'red clay'. But
the redness of this primal vitality is also the redness of violence, the
fall from the pole of *forma* toward the pole of *materia* which ends as
a descent into materialism; this is one reason why it was adopted by

the 'reds', the Marxists. And it is not Isaac's first-born son Esau—God's original creative impulse—who receives the blessing, but his younger son Jacob, symbol of *tikkun*, the reversal of the cosmogonic process, otherwise knows as the spiritual Path. The exhaustion of the tears of Esau represents the exhaustion of materialism, the termination of the impulse to run after the lost Paradise into the wilderness of matter, energy, space and time. In metaphysical terms, it is the exhaustion of the current of creative manifestation for this cycle.

Rabbi Israel of Rizhin said: In the days of the Messiah man will no longer quarrel with his fellow but with himself. The struggle with the outer world will be superseded by the struggle to conquer the inner world; in Muslim terms, the Lesser Jihad will give way to the Greater. (W.B. Yeats also, in *A Vision*, predicted that the coming age would be 'antithetical' as the one passing away was 'primary'. The primary character, or humanity in primary ages, battles with conditions, while the antithetical character, or man in antithetical ages, battles with himself.) Rabbi Israel also said that the Messianic world will be a world without images, 'in which the image and its object can no longer be related.' In negative terms, in terms of the 'generation totally corrupt,' this indicates the solipsistic nadir of postmodernism, where all experiences are considered to be without objective referent—mere images. In the positive terms of 'a generation wholly innocent,' it refers to the *tikkun* or reabsorption of all things into their invisible and transcendent principles. If image and object, or *phenomenon* and *noumenon*, or cosmic manifestation and its Divine Source, can no longer be 'related' as two separate terms, it means that they are either totally divorced or totally united. The former state is Hell; the latter is Paradise; the final separation between the divorced condition and the married condition is the Last Judgement.

MAITREYA:
BUDDHIST ESCHATOLOGY

In most schools of Buddhism, the future Buddha—either the last Buddha of this cycle of manifestation, or simply the next Buddha to appear—will be named Maitreya, a word which means 'moonlight' (It may or may not be significant that the Prophet Muhammad, considered as perfectly receptive to the light of Allah, is also compared to the moon.) In *Maitreya, The Future Buddha* [ed. Alan Sponberg and Helen Hardacre, Cambridge University Press, 1988], my main authority for this exposition, contributor Jan Nattier calls Maitreya the 'anointed' heir of Shakyamuni, the historical figure we know as 'the Buddha'. He would therefore be, at least in the narrow etymological sense, a *messiah* or *christ*, which in Hebrew and Greek respectively mean 'anointed one'—though Nattier may simply be using the word 'anointed' in a loose, generic sense. His name may well relate him to the Zoroastrian savior Mithra; Joseph M. Kitagawa, in the same book, draws parallels between Maitreya and the Zoroastrian Saoshyant.

The Buddhist doctrine of cyclical time is notoriously a-historical, generating predictions like 'a few thousand years from now the human life-span will have increased to 80,000 years,' a statement which clearly can only have a symbolic or mythological meaning. And where the Hindu doctrine of cycles usually accepted by the Traditionalists, via Coomaraswamy and Guénon, begins with a Golden Age, descends through Silver, Bronze, and Iron ages, then ends with an apocalyptic dissolution, after which a new Golden Age descends fully-formed from the heavenly worlds, the Buddhists view cyclical time more horizontally, as a rising and falling of vast aeonic waves; the cosmic environment gradually sinks in its ability to receive the truth, and then gradually rises. The Hindu doctrine of cycles is substantially the same as that of the classical Greeks, and roughly in line with Christian and Muslim eschatology; the Buddhist doctrine is shared by the Jains, and was more-or-less the one adopted by the Theosophical Society, except for the fact that the Buddhist place the next Golden Age thousands of years in the future (roughly 2,500 years according to some schools, though certain teachers now tend to shorten this to 500 years, given the degeneracy of the times), whereas H. P. Blavatsky in *The Secret Doctrine* saw it as imminent.

Be that as it may, most Buddhists agree with traditional Christians, Muslims and Hindus that our present age is on a downward course. We are in the 'last 500 years of the dharma,' the final period of the cycle at the end of which Buddhism will die out, or live on only as a empty shadow of its former self. The age itself will end in war before the appearance of Maitreya, just as, in Christian eschatology, Armageddon will precede the Second Coming of Christ. Many, such as Martin Lings, identify Maitreya with the Hindu Kalki, the 10th and last avatar of Vishnu, who will come at the end of the degenerate Kali-yuga to end this cycle and inaugurate a new one, particularly in view of the fact that the Hindu scripture the *Bhavagata Purana* identifies the ninth avatar of Vishnu with the historical Buddha. The Theravadins view Maitreya as the last of the five Buddhas of the present time- period, which, though it will end with the degeneration of Buddhism, is seen as 'the good eon', as opposed to the Hindu understanding of our time as the Kali-yuga, and Age of Iron. The Mahayana Buddhists, on the other hand, usually assign Maitreya to the far distant Golden Age of the next cycle, when the world will have finally recovered from the degeneration and apocalyptic end of this one; he does not inaugurate this cycle but only enters it when the time is ripe. This Mahayana version of Maitreya could therefore be called 'post-millennialist', though not in the progressivist or reformist sense, since Buddhism sees its cycles of spiritual flowering and degeneration more as the seasons of a pre-established pattern than as the product of human action or its abdication. The fruits of karma ripen more to the spiritual advancement or retardation of the individual than to the worsening or betterment of the world. Some Mahayana Buddhists however, particularly in China and Southeast Asia, have envisioned Maitreya as destined to appear in this very 'final 500 years of the dharma,' perhaps even within the present generation, seeing him as a revolutionary/apocalyptic figure similar to Christ or the Mahdi or the Jewish Messiah— a system of beliefs which, as in the case of analogous doctrines within the Abrahamic religions, has tended to produce dynastic struggles or popular liberation movements headed by quasi-religious 'pretenders' claiming to be the expected Buddhist Savior.

Maitreya will appear during the reign of a world monarch, a *chakravartin* ('turner of the wheel'). Jan Nattier repeats the prophecy that he will be announced by Kashyapa, a disciple of Shakyamuni who has remained in suspended animation through the ages until the time when he will emerge as herald of Maitreya. (Nattier hears in 'Kashyapa' the Persian name of 'Keresaspa', the designated herald of the Zoroastrian savior Saoshyant. Keresaspa will also emerge from 'occultation' or suspended animation to play his role.) According to the Tendai School, he will be a Singhalese king by the name of Dhutta-Gamani, brother to Maitreya and also his first disciple. Others give the king's name as Shanka. According to one story, he will renounce his throne in order to follow Maitreya. Since Shanka will necessarily be of the kingly-warrior caste, a *kshatriya*, Maitreya—unlike Gautama, who was also a *kshatriya*—will be of the highest priestly caste, a *brahmin*. Such a conjunction between a Buddha and a *chakravartin* takes place very rarely; according to the Mahayana lore recounted by Padmanabh S. Jaini, in his chapter 'The Stages in the Bodhisattva Career of Tathagata Maitreya', it only occurs 'at the start of each new ascension within an intermediate eon (*antarkalpa*) in a given time cycle (*mahakalpa*).' We are now 'at the tail end of an *antarkalpa*, which is moving rapidly toward a minor apocalypse.' Thus Maitreya will incarnate in the far distant future, in a new civilization supported by 'two wheels of the law', the wheel of merit leading to Paradise, turned by a *chakravartin*, and the wheel of renunciation leading to Nirvana, turned by himself as Buddha. This would appear to be the Buddhist version of the Hindu *satyayuga* or Golden Age, when worldly abundance and otherworldly bliss are not the opponents of final Liberation, as they often must be for us in this Age of Iron, but rather the disciples of it.

THE PAROUSIA:
CHRISTIAN ESCHATOLOGY

There is so much contemporary Christian literature relating to the latter days and the apocalypse, especially from the Evangelical wing of the church, that instead of trying to make sense of that profusion I will simply draw on what has fallen effortlessly into my hands. My wife's conversion to Russian Orthodoxy has added many new books to our shelves, among which are *The Apocalypse of St John: An Orthodox Commentary* by Archbishop Averky of Jordanville, based on many patristic sources (notably the *Commentary on the Apocalypse* by St Andrew, Archbishop of Caesaria, c. 5th century) and *Ultimate Things: An Orthodox Christian Perspective on the End Times*, by Dennis E. Engleman, which was recommended to us by Rama Coomaraswamy. Both books have the advantage of being largely based on the earliest Christian sources, and both walk the fine line between an over-literal and an over-allegorical interpretation of scripture. They are perfectly timely, but not so tied to the daily news that they run the risk of being trampled by the course of events. Much of this section is based on the above two books, supplemented by Guénon's *The Reign of Quantity and the Signs of the Times*.

The Orthodox interpretation of the *Apocalypse* and its doctrine of eschatology in general departs from many Evangelical interpretations in two major ways. First, it is firmly a-millennial. Christ will not come to establish a thousand-year earthly reign after the tribulation, as in pre-millennialism, nor will he descend to crown a thousand-year rule of Christendom established by his followers, as in post-millennialism. Such millennialism was condemned, as the heresy of 'chiliasm', by the Second Ecumenical Council. For most Orthodox, as well as for St Augustine and most traditional Catholics, the 'millennium' described in Rev. 20:1–10, when Satan shall be bound, is the church age itself, and is largely past.

In my own opinion, the placing of the millennium after the eschatological combat, which has led many into interpreting it as a worldly Christian empire of the future, has to do with the secret correspondence between the Church Militant and the Church

Triumphant. If Christ's kingdom is 'not of this world', and if membership in it is based on one's dying with Christ and so participating in His resurrection, then Christians are in one sense beyond the Apocalypse already, dwelling in a heavenly 'millennium' which will have no end.

The second main departure from Evangelical eschatology has to do with the materialistic interpretation of 'the rapture', a notion based, according to Engleman, on the visions of a Scotswoman, Margaret Macdonald, in 1830. The supporters of this doctrine cite Rev. 3:10, 'I also will keep you from the hour of trial which shall come upon the whole world,' as well as 1 Thess. 4:15–17, according to which the living in Christ shall be 'caught up . . . in the clouds to meet the Lord in the air,' and Matt. 24:29–31, when the angels shall gather together the elect 'from the four winds, from one end of heaven to the other.' According to Engleman, this has nothing to do with a levitation or dematerialization of Christians so they can escape the tribulation, but with an 'instantaneous spiritual transformation.' In support of this he cites John 17:15: 'I do not pray that You should take them out of the world, but that You should keep them from the evil one.'

In my own opinion, since in I Thessalonians the living are to be caught up *after* the resurrection of the dead, to meet them in the air, this may also simply refer to the entry of the saved into heaven after death. In any case, it has nothing to do with a special dispensation to Christians allowing them to escape the great tribulation, since it will happen after the tribulation has ended. Engleman and other Orthodox Christians believe that the Evangelical expectation of an earthly millennium, and the belief that Christians will escape the tribulation, are precisely the erroneous doctrines which will lead many of them to mistake Antichrist and his earthly rule for Christ and his Kingdom. And, I would add, the doctrine of the rapture is in part responsible for the contemporary fascination with 'alien abductions'. (The hippy version of the rapture was that all the good hippies would be taken away to a new world in the alien 'mothership'.)

Engleman quotes St Augustine's summary of Christian eschatology from *The City of God*:

Elias the Tishbite shall come; the Jews shall believe; Antichrist shall persecute; Christ shall judge; the dead shall rise; the good and the wicked shall be separated; the world shall be burned and renewed.

And while he accepts the Apocalypse as both a spiritual and a future historical event, Augustine cautions against taking its symbols too literally, and especially against setting dates, since 'of that day and hour no one knows, not even the angels in heaven, but my Father only' (Matt. 24: 36).

The four beasts in the Book of Daniel which come up out of the sea Engleman interprets as four world empires. The last beast, with ten horns, three of which are torn out to make room for a little horn 'speaking pompous words' is interpreted as Rome, which is extended to cover the several world empires which arose out of Western Christendom, including the coming New World Order. According to St Hippolytus, the 'little horn' is Antichrist. The fourth beast is analogous to the Beast of the *Apocalypse*, having seven heads and ten horns, which many see as seven successive kingdoms and ten contemporary kings. The sea from which the four beasts in *Daniel* and the Beast of the *Apocalypse* emerge is interpreted as the tempestuous sea of collective humanity. (I tend to see it more as the 'collective unconscious', the mass psychological condition of the fallen human soul, which comes to essentially the same thing. As the 'sea' is mass psychology, so the 'air' is the psychic plane *per se*, inhabited by those subtle beings called in the Bible 'the powers of the air', who are generally considered demonic.)

The global empire of the fourth beast in *Daniel* will be the base of operations for Antichrist. The Jews will return to their homeland. The Temple will be restored. In it the Antichrist will be acknowledged by the Jews as their Messiah, and later as God. Most of Christendom will abandon its doctrines to follow him.

The end times will be times of mass apostasy and demonic deception. Such apostasy cannot be stopped; the best one can do is avoid being influenced by it, which in itself will be a kind of life-or-death struggle. When the Antichrist arises, it is time to return to the catacomb church, since the 'above-ground' church, even Orthodoxy itself, will for the most part worship him.

If Satan is the ape of God, Antichrist can be called the ape of Christ. He will counterfeit the life experiences and miracles of Christ, even, as far as possible, the resurrection. Like Christ, he will be a teacher. He will be a king of this world, as Christ is a monarch of a kingdom not of this world; he will be a high priest of all religions, requiring that all men worship him as God. He will begin his reign with a show of mildness, which will quickly become a reign of terror. He will deceive many—including himself, according to some, since he will not know that he is really Antichrist.

The symbol for both Christ and Antichrist, according to St Hippolytus, is the lion. (It's an interesting fact that the god *Legba*, the 'Christ' of the Voudoo religion, is also symbolized by the lion.) As Guénon says in *The Reign of Quantity*,

> the Antichrist can adopt the very symbols of the Messiah, using them of course in an inverted sense. . . . In the same way there can be and must be a strange resemblance between the designations of the Messiah (*al-masīḥ* in Arabic) and of the Antichrist (*al-masīkh*). . . . *Masīkh* can be taken as a deformation of *Masīḥa*, by the mere addition of a dot to the final letter; but at the same time the first word means 'deformed', which correctly expresses the character of the Antichrist.' (p 272 and n173).

In the early 1800s, St Nilus revealed that Antichrist would be born 'without man's sowing'—by artificial insemination or genetic manipulation, presumably—from the womb of an evil woman; his emergence will thus be a satanic counterfeit of the virgin birth of Jesus. In Guénon's words (*The Reign of Quantity*, p 273),

> the false is necessarily also the 'artificial', and in this respect the 'counter-tradition' cannot fail, despite its other characteristics, to retain the 'mechanical' character appertaining to all the productions of the modern world, of which it will itself be the last.

According to St Hippolytus, the mother of Antichrist will come from the Tribe of Dan, the only tribe of Israel not mentioned in the *Apocalypse*, and which is called (in Gen. 49:17) 'a serpent by the way, a viper by the path.' (The serpent-god of Voudoo, *Danbhala*, is perhaps related to the Tribe of Dan, especially since one of the many tributaries to the magical syncretism of Voudoo was a heterodox form of Ethiopian Judaism. The place of Dan, among the regions in Palestine assigned to the tribes of Israel, is in the North, which may indicate that he, like the serpent in Eden, has something to do with the fall of the Hyperborean Paradise.)

The number of the Beast, 666 (Rev. 13:18), is interpreted (*Ultimate Things*, p140) as follows: While 7 is the number of God, Who transcends manifestation, 6 is the number of complete manifestation. Therefore 666 refers to 'the kingdom of man and nature without God' extended into the realms of body, mind and soul. (Guénon, in *The Reign of Quantity*, [chap. 39, n7] says that 'the number of the Beast' is also a solar number—another example of the 'ape of Christ' principle, since Christ is 'the Sun of Righteousness'.) The Image of the Beast in Rev. 13, which the second beast who is the False Prophet causes to be set up and worshipped by all men, is identified with the image with gold head, silver chest, bronze belly, iron legs, and feet of iron mixed with clay dreamt of by King Nebuchadnezzar (Dan. 2:31–44), which falls after having its feet broken by 'the stone not cut by hands'—the Kingdom of God— and further identified with the idol of gold set up by the king to be worshipped by all men in *Daniel* 3. The different metals represent four world empires from Babylon to Rome; the Image of the Beast is thus the totality of the kingdom of man set up against the kingdom of God. (The Traditionalist writers identify the image in *Daniel* with the four world ages in Greco-Roman and Hindu traditions. The fact that the feet of the image are partially of clay refers to the ontological instability of the end times. The final destiny of materialism, symbolized by iron which seems so strong and permanent, is dissolution, since matter is the most instable and ephemeral of all things. The abandonment of the concept of solid matter by modern physics, and the fragmentation of our image of the material world by the electronic media, are clear signs of this dissolution.)

The Antichrist, according to the *Apocalypse*, will rule for 'seven days' which are really seven years, though even this period of time should not be taken too literally.

According to Engleman, he will rise to power in a politically unified world. His capital will be Jerusalem, his seat a renewed Jewish

Temple. (Conservative Jews in Israel are prepared even now to rebuild the Temple, and believe that the one who leads them to rebuild it will be the Messiah.)

The Prophets Enoch and Elias, the 'two witnesses' of Rev. 11:3–5, will then return and denounce the Antichrist. (According to the Old Testament, neither Enoch nor Elias experienced death, which is why the Sufis identify Elias with Khidr the 'immortal prophet'.) They will be martyred by Antichrist, rise again after three and one-half days, and ascend into heaven. Because of their ministry, a remnant of the Jews will be converted to Christ.

After the martyrdom of the witnesses, the Tribulation will begin. The Beast will place his mark upon all who submit to him, without which none can buy or sell. The world will be enslaved. The great end-time plagues will come. The Temple will be desolated. And Christians everywhere will be persecuted.

According to the *Apocalypse* and *Zechariah*, the final battle will be fought in the valley of Armageddon near Jerusalem. Satan will deceive the nations, Gog and Magog (Rev. 20:7–9) and gather them together for battle, where they will be destroyed by fire from heaven. The greatest earthquake in the history of the earth will take place. The Euphrates river will dry up. The Archangel Michael will go to war with the dragon (Satan) 'in heaven', defeat him, and cast him out (Rev. 12:7–9).

Then Christ, Word of God, will come down from heaven. With his angelic armies he will war against the Beast, the False Prophet and their armies, triumph over them, and cast them into the lake of fire (Rev. 19:11–21). The Heavenly Jerusalem will descend. The dead will rise and be judged. There will be a new heaven and a new earth.

The *Apocalypse* contains one fascinating episode which I've never heard anyone comment upon. Rev. 17:16–17 reads as follows:

> And the ten horns which thou sawest upon the beast, these shall hate the whore, and shall make her desolate and naked, and shall eat of her flesh, and burn her with fire.

> For God hath put it into their hearts to fulfill his will, and to agree, and give their kingdoms unto the beast, until the words of God shall be fulfilled.

On the face of it, this seems to say that the Antichrist himself, or the ten horns upon his head, who are his servants the ten kings, will destroy the Whore of Babylon. First the Whore is seen riding on the beast (Rev. 17:3); but then the ten kings slay her, after which— according to God's will—they turn their kingdoms over to the beast. What are we to make of this?

Perhaps it refers to a time of luxury and over-indulgence which gives way to a time of harshness, and which seems by its very degeneracy to justify that harshness, as the decadence of the Weimar Republic lent credibility to Hitler's draconian measures. It may also picture a unified world economy whose breakup, due to internal contradictions, resurgent nationalism or other factors, ushers in the reign of Antichrist, who alone seems capable of restoring order.

THE IMAM MAHDI AND THE PROPHET JESUS: MUSLIM ESCHATOLOGY

My main source for this section is *Islamic Messianism: The Idea of the Mahdi in Twelver Shi'ism*, by Abdulaziz Abdulhussein Sachedina. *Sachedina's primary sources are Muhammad ibn Ali al-Baqir and Jafar al-Sadiq, the 5th and 6th Shiïte Imams*

The signs of the Hour of Judgement in Islamic tradition are many. The moon will be split in two, symbolizing the breaching of the psychic isthmus between this material 'sublunary' world and the next world, the barrier between time and eternity. (The disappearance of the sea at the coming of the new heaven and the new earth in Rev. 21:1 undoubtedly has the same meaning; the sea is unstable and ever-shifting like the psyche, and the moon rules the sea.) According to a *hadith* of the Prophet, buildings will reach the sky as the end approaches, and men will dress like women. (Interestingly, St Nilus of Mount Athos, in the 19th century, also mentioned cross-dressing as an apocalyptic sign; and I would add that since polarity is the principle of all cosmic manifestation, the erosion of sexual differences is a clear sign of the dissolution of earthly humanity.) Among other signs, the Koran predicts a great earthquake (Surah

'The Earthquake'), like the one described in Rev. 16:18. Surah (96), 'The Prophets', speaks of a time when 'Gog and Magog are unloosed, and they slide down out of every slope, and nigh has drawn the true promise'; the same Surah makes reference to a 'beast' which will come 'out of the earth' in the latter days and speak to men 'when the Word falls on them.' According to one *hadith,* which sounds like a version of the modern Evangelical Christian idea of the Rapture, 'God will send a cold wind from the direction of Syria'—the North—'and no one who has in his heart as much as a single grain of good shall remain in the earth without being taken.' (Compare Matt. 24:40–4 and 1 Thess. 4:17; also *The Siege of Shambhala,* below.)

Islamic eschatology shares with Christianity the belief that Jesus will return at the end of time. Muslims, however, who call Jesus 'the Spirit of God' and even accept the doctrine of the virgin birth, still see him as a great prophet but not the Son of God since, according to the Koran, God 'neither begets nor is He begotten.'

Along with the second coming of Jesus, Muslims also expect the advent of the Mahdi, the 'rightly-guided one', whom the Shiites identify with Muhammad al-Mahdi, the occulted Twelfth Imam. The doctrine of the Mahdi is much more highly developed in Shiism, where it has achieved dogmatic status, than in Sunni Islam; some Sunnis, in reaction against the Shiite conception, even repeat the tradition that 'There is no Mahdi save Jesus, the Son of Mary.' Nonetheless, according to the great Muslim historian, Ibn Khaldun, from his *Muqaddima,*

It has been well known (and generally accepted) by all Muslims in every epoch, that at the end of time a man from the family (of the Prophet) will without fail make his appearance, one who will strengthen Islam and make justice triumph. Muslims will follow him, and he will gain domination over the Muslim realm. He will be called the Mahdi. Following him, the Antichrist will appear, together with all the subsequent signs of the Hour.[4]

4. *Islamic Messianism,* p14.

The Mahdi will appear 'after hearts become hard and the earth is filled with wickedness' (cf. Matt. 24:10–12). According to the *hadith* of Muhammad, 'no one will more resemble me than al-Mahdi.' He will 'fill the earth with equity and justice, even as it has been filled with inequity, injustice and tyranny.' He will appear in the end times, when the sun rises in the West. Another sign of his advent will be an eclipse of the sun in the middle of Ramadan and of the moon at the end—an astronomical impossibility. He will come during the *fitan* ('trials'), sedition and civil strife, the tribulation of the latter days. The descent of Jesus during the rule of al-Mahdi will be the sign of the Hour.

According to Sunni sources, Jesus will slay the Antichrist:

> He will descend to the Holy Land at a place called Afiq with a spear in his hand; he will kill with it al-Dajjal and go to Jerusalem at the time of the morning prayer. The Imam will seek to yield his place to him, but Jesus will refuse and will worship behind him according to the Shari'a of Muhammad. Thereafter he will kill the swine, break the cross, and kill all the Christians who do not believe in him. Once al-Dajjal is killed, the Peoples of the Book will believe in him and will form one single *umma* of those who submit to the will of God. Jesus will establish the rule of justice and will remain for forty years, after which he will die. His funeral will take place in Medina, where he will be buried beside Muhammad, in a place between Abu Bakr and 'Umar'.[5]

Like the Christ of the *Apocalypse*, al-Qaim al-Mahdi ('he who rises up, the rightly-guided') will embody the principle of inflexible justice, rather than the quality of severity tempered with diplomacy and mercy exhibited by the Prophet Muhammad (upon whom be peace). According to Shiite sources, he will inherit the Prophet's coat of mail, his short spear, and his sword, *Dhu al-Fiqar* (meaning either 'two-pointed' or 'doubly piercing'), which he gave to Ali ibn abi-Talib. In the Shiite version, al-Mahdi, not Jesus, will slay the Antichrist.

5. *Islamic Messianism*, pp 171–172.

According to a tradition of Ali, the emergence of Antichrist or *al-Dajjal* will be preceded by a time of great hardship, a 'tribulation'. On his forehead will be written 'This is the *kafir* ('non-believer'), which everyone, literate or illiterate, will be able to read. Like Jesus, he will ride on a donkey. He will sound a call which will be heard from one end of the earth to the other. He will claim to be God. On the day of his emergence, his followers will be wearing something green on their heads. In a place named Afiq (just as in the Sunni account) in Syria, on a Friday, three hours before sunset, God will cause him and his followers to be killed by 'the one behind whom Jesus shall worship'—the Twelfth Imam, the Mahdi. This will be the beginning of the great revolution of the Imam—the one counter-feited in 1979 by the Ayatollah Khomeini—after which no repen-tance will be accepted (pp172–173).

According to a *hadith* of Jafar al-Sadiq, the Mahdi will enter Mecca with a yellow turban on his head and driving a herd of goats. He will be wearing the Prophet's patched sandals and carrying his staff. He will appear as a youth. He will proceed to the Kaaba, where he will be met during the night by Michael, Gabriel and a host of angels. He will stand between the hills Rukn and Maqam, announce himself, and demand allegiance. The people will assemble. Then God will cause four pillars of light to rise into the heavens; everyone on earth will see them, and know that al-Qaim has emerged. Imam al-Hussein (the Prophet's grandson, the Second Imam), wearing a black turban, and 12,000 *shi'a* of Ali will rise from the dead; (anyone who makes obeisance to al-Hussein before the rise of al-Qaim is an infidel). Al- Qaim al-Mahdi will lean his back against the wall of the Kaaba and extend his hand, from which a light will shine out. The first of many to make obeisance to him will be Gabriel, followed by the faithful among the *jinn*, the nobles of Mecca and others.

All this will happen at sunrise. After the sun has climbed higher, a voice from the East will announce that the Mahdi has come. The whole earth will hear it. But at sundown, a second voice will cry from the West, announcing the coming of an Ummayad 'anti-Mahdi'. Many will be led astray by this call.

The Mahdi will reveal the true text of the scriptures of Adam and Seth, Noah and Abraham, as well as the Torah, the Psalms and the

Gospel. The followers of these scriptures will acknowledge that he has restored them to their true form, as they were before the texts were distorted. Then he will read the Koran, and its followers will acknowledge that nothing whatever had been distorted in the text of the Book. He will tear down the Kaaba and rebuild it as it was in Adam's time. He will fight against the unbelievers and slay them. He will kill al-Sufyan, the Ummayad false messiah (who may or may not be the same figure as the earlier one I have called the 'anti-Mahdi'.) Ali will return from the dead to dwell in a huge tent, as big as a whole country, supported on four pillars. Heaven and earth will be illuminated. All secrets will be revealed (pp161–166).

William C. Chittick, in *Islamic Spirituality I*, gives an esoteric commentary by the Sufi Al-Jili from his *Al-Insan al-kamil*, dealing with some of the scripture passages and traditions relating to the Hour of Judgement:

> Al-Jili interprets the events that take place at the end of time in terms of the voluntary death or Greatest resurrection experienced by the spiritual traveler. According to a *hadith*, Gog and Magog will appear on earth, eating its fruits and drinking its seas; once they are slain, the earth will revive. In the same way the ego's agitation and corrupt thoughts take possession of the earth of a man's heart, eat its fruits and drink its seas, so that no trace of spiritual knowledge can appear. Then God's angels annihilate these satanic whisperings with sciences from God: the earth is revived and it gives abundant harvest. This is a mark of man's gaining proximity to God. As for the beast of the earth, it will come to tell the earth's inhabitants about the truths of the promises concerning the resurrection. In the same way, the traveler reaches a stage of unveiling where he comes to understand the inward mysteries of religion; this is a favor from God, so that 'the troops of his faith will not retreat before the armies of the continuing veil.' Just as the people will not be convinced of the coming of the Hour until the appearance of the beast, so the gnostic will not understand all the requisites of Divinity until the spirit appears from out of the earth of his bodily nature. The conflict between al-Dajjal and Jesus refers to the battle between

the ego and the spirit, while the appearance of the Mahdi alludes to man's becoming 'the Possessor of Equilibrium at the pinnacle of every perfection.' Finally, the rising of the sun from the West marks the realization of the ultimate human perfection (p 401).

Several Surahs of the Koran deal with the Hour of Judgement, among them 'The Overthrowing' (81), 'The Cleaving' (82), 'The Sundering' (84), 'The Earthquake' (99), and 'The Calamity' (101). Here are some relevant passages which, like most of the Koran, can be interpreted both in terms of outward events and of inward spiritual transformation:

From *The Cleaving*:

In the name of Allah, the Beneficent, the Merciful
When the heaven is cleft asunder,
When the planets are dispersed,
When the sea is poured forth,
And the sepulchres are overturned,
A soul will know what it hath sent before (it) and what
left behind . . .

From *The Overthrowing*:

When the Sun is overthrown,
And when the stars fall,
And when the hills are moved,
And when the camels big with young are abandoned,
And when the wild beasts are herded together,
And when the seas rise,
And when the souls are reunited,
And when the girl-child that was buried alive is asked
For what sin she was slain,
And when the pages are laid open,
And when the sky is torn away,
And when hell is lighted,
And when the garden is brought nigh,
(Then) every soul will know what it hath made ready . . .

From *The Sundering*:

When the heaven is split asunder,
And attentive to her Lord in fear,
When the earth is spread out
And hath cast out all that was in her, and is empty,
And attentive to her Lord in fear!
Thou, verily, O man, art working toward thy Lord a
work which thou shalt meet (in His presence)....
.... I swear by the afterglow of sunset
And by the night and all that it enshroudeth,
And by the moon when she is at the full,
That ye shall journey on from plane to plane.
What aileth them, then, that they believe not?

CHRISTIAN AND MUSLIM
ESCHATOLOGY COMPARED

As we have already seen, there are many parallels between Muslim
and Christian eschatological lore. Martin Lings, in *The Eleventh
Hour*, quotes the Sunni tradition of the Prophet, that

A body of my people will not cease to fight for the truth until the
coming forth of the Antichrist.... When they are pressing on to
fight, even while they straighten their lines for the prayer when it
is called, Jesus the son of Mary will descend and will lead them in
prayer. And the enemy of God, when he seeth Jesus, will melt
even as salt melteth in water. If he were let be, he would melt into
perishing: but God will slay him at the hand of Jesus, who will
show them his blood upon his lance.

Given the undeniable difference in levels, the slaying of Antichrist
by Jesus obviously parallels the story told in many Orthodox icons
of St Michael, where the archangel is shown in the act of slaying the
Antichrist—with a lance. Furthermore, when the Mahdi manifests
himself at the Kaaba, according to the Shiïte tradition of Jafar al-
Sadiq, the Sixth Imam (see above), he receives obeisance not only

from the faithful, but from the angels and the Jinn; thus al-Mahdi, like St Michael, is also the leader of the 'heavenly host'. (Jafar recounts another tradition that the false Ummayad messiah will also be slain by an archangel, not by Michael, however, but by Gabriel.) In the Shiïte traditions, as we have seen, it is not Jesus' role but the Mahdi's to kill the Antichrist, also with a lance. The title of the Mahdi, *sahib al-sayf*, 'master of the sword', connects him with the Kalki Avatara (see below) in the *Bhagavata Purana* and also with the Christ of Rev. 19:12; 21, and who says of himself in the Gospels that 'I come not to bring peace, but a sword.' Is the 'two-edged sword' of Jesus Christ in the *Apocalypse* related to *Dhu'l Fiqar,* the two-pointed sword wielded by both the Prophet Muhammad and the Imam Ali, upon whom be peace?

The Orthodox icons of St George and St Michael seem to present Michael as the angelic archetype of George, who is his active agent in this world. Both employ the lance. As Michael kills the Antichrist, so George kills the Dragon, which, in the Apocalypse, symbolizes Satan, whom the Antichrist serves. Muslims venerate St George as identical with the Sufi immortal prophet Khidr, whom Sufis also identify with Elias. According to the book of Malachi, as well as the Gospels, Elias is supposed to come to restore all things before the great and terrible Day of the Lord. Leo Schaya identifies Elias with the Mahdi.

Lings recounts the *hadith* that the Antichrist will be 'a man blind in his right eye, in which all light is extinguished, even as it were a grape.' In a tradition of Ali, the Antichrist's single eye is 'in the center of his forehead, shining like a star'—which is paralleled by an apocalyptic vision of St John of Kronstadt, where he was conducted in the spirit by St Seraphim of Sarov through scenes of the coming of the Antichrist. In one scene, Antichrist sits enthroned on the altar in Jerusalem, presumably in the Church of the Holy Sepulchre—though the Dome of the Rock or a restored Jewish Temple are also possible interpretations—wearing 'a golden crown with a star'. (*Divine Ascent, A Journal of Orthodox Faith,* vol. 1, no. 1.)

The fact that Antichrist only has sight in the left eye signifies, according to the Sufi Najmo-d Din Razi, that he is a materialist, aware of this world but blind to the next. His perception is cut off from the higher spiritual worlds; he recognizes nothing beyond the world of the senses. (A similar truth is expressed in Eastern Orthodox icons, where Satan is always shown in profile, with only one eye visible: sin involves a lack of perspective.) But the tradition that the single eye of Antichrist is in the center of his forehead, shining like a star, has a different significance. The star in the forehead is a representation of the *ajña-chakra*, the 'third eye', which is the organ of subtle or spiritual insight. This means that the Antichrist will be capable up to a point of co-opting and perverting the faculties of higher perception, possibly only on the subtle level of 'remote viewing' and the like, but possibly also on the level of a mental understanding of metaphysical truth, or even that of a frigid indifference playing the part of a high spiritual detachment—a cold, heartless contemplation of the 'existential nakedness' of things masquerading as a deep contemplation of pure Being. It may ultimately be true that the only level of consciousness totally immune from perversion will be the 'cardiac' consciousness which the Sufis, and the Hindus, and the Eastern Orthodox Christians call the 'Heart', the level of the Image of God within us, whose inner core—the 'eye of the Heart'—is the Divine Witness, the *atman*. The 'rapture' which protects God's elect from the tribulation brought on by the Antichrist may, on one level of meaning, be an absorption into the 'paradise of the Heart' when all else in society and the human soul has been invaded by darkness. St Augustine, in *The City of God*, defines demonic evil as *knowledge without love*—which can never be the highest form of knowledge, the knowledge of the *logoi*, the prototypes of all things as they exist in the mind of God; this degree of knowledge, he implies, cannot exist without love. When demonic lovelessness invades the head, the only refuge is the Heart—which does *not* mean that the only protection from perverted thinking is intense emotion. The Antichrist is equally capable of perverting emotion, which is perhaps one of the symbolic meanings of the Whore of Babylon. The strategy is not to abandon the head and hide in the Heart, but to 'sever the head'—which is a Sufi symbol for overcoming the 'headstrong' ego—and place it, as it were, within the Heart. In other words, knowledge must deepen, until it is no longer my little individual attempt to understand the world and the God Who made it, but God's eternal creative act of Self-witnessing within me, and, through me, within the mirror of the world, since it is ultimately this Divine Act of Self-witnessing which creates both self and world.

The star-crowned Antichrist is a counterfeit of Christ, whose birth was announced by a star; this is another example of the parallel symbology between Christ and Antichrist. Rev. 2:28 says, 'And I will give [him who overcomes] the morning star.' According to Archbishop Averky in *The Apocalypse of St John: An Orthodox Commentary*, this means either that he will receive Christ, who in 2 Peter 1:19 is called 'the morning star' that shines in the hearts of men, or that he will receive dominion over Satan, who in Isaiah 14:12 is identified with Lucifer, the morning star.

The one-eyed nature of Antichrist represents a counterfeit of the Divine Unity. When Jesus said, 'If your eye become single, your whole body shall be filled with light,' he was referring to the Eye of the Heart which witnesses the Unity of God, and transmits the light of that Unity to the individual psyche, from the psyche to the body, and from the body to the universe, which is thereby restored to its Edenic state, where the world presented to us by our senses is experienced as the primordial mirror of the Names or Energies of God. But the single eye of the Antichrist can only see and worship the universe as if it literally *were* God, mystifying and glamorizing matter for the purpose of denying the Divine Transcendence, in the manner of anti-religious materialists like Carl Sagan. Those who seek unity and stability through the worship of matter will, however, find themselves worshipping chaos instead. In the words of the Gospels, they are those whose 'house is founded on sand,' on a swarm of sub-atomic particles ruled by random indeterminacy, as well as on the chaos of mass 'atomic individualism' which is the social expression of this vision of things. The only source of stability, the only 'rock', is the Divine Nature, where the radiant eternal forms or *logoi* of all things rest in the mind of God.

According to Shiite tradition, the Twelfth Imam Muhammad al-Mahdi was 'occulted' (hidden away) in childhood to prevent his assassination, reminding one of Rev. 12:1–5, where the 'woman clothed with the sun' gives birth to a 'man child', who was to 'rule all nations with a rod of iron,' but who was 'caught up to God, and to His throne' to avoid being devoured by 'a great red dragon having seven heads and ten horns.' World chaos will be among the signs of his imminent return. When he does, the mothers nursing their infants will abandon them in fear; cf. Matt. 24:19, 'And woe to those that are with child, and to them that give suck in those days!' It is unlawful to mention (or reveal) the name of al-Mahdi, or ask his whereabouts, of fix the time of his advent, though many traditions say it will be in the 'near future'. Compare Rev. 19:11–12, where the rider on the white horse, called Faithful and True 'had a name written that no man knew, but He Himself,' and Matt. 24:26, 'if they shall say unto you, Behold, he is in the desert; go not forth: behold, he is in the secret chambers; believe it not,' as well as Matt. 24:36, 'But of that day and hour knoweth no man, no, not the angels of heaven, but my Father only.' Compare also Rev. 22:7: 'Behold, I come quickly,' and Rev. 3:12–13, 'I will write upon [him that overcometh] my new name.'

The Mahdi will also bring a new Book; compare Rev. 5:1–2, 'And I saw in the right hand of him that sat on the throne a book written within and on the backside, sealed with seven seals. And I saw a strong angel proclaiming with a loud voice, Who is worthy to open the book, and to loose the seals thereof?'; compare also the *Sepher ha-Yasher* or Book of Justice which, according to Jewish tradition, will be brought by Elias in the latter days (see below). And just as we are warned in Matt. 24:24–27 not to run after false Christs and false prophets on hearsay, 'For as the lightning cometh out of the East, and shineth even to the West; so shall the coming of the Son of Man be,' so the greatest authority in Shiïte Islam, the Sixth Imam Jafar al-Sadiq, declares 'Beware, those who claim [that the Mahdi has come] before the rise of al-Sufyani [the Ummayad false messiah, similar to Antichrist] and the voice from the sky are liars.'

An interesting parallel, which is also a clear divergence, between the Koran and the *Apocalypse*, has to do with a beast which shall rise out of the earth in the latter days. In Islamic tradition, Antichrist emerges from the earth; in Christian tradition, from the sea. (Certain Islamic versions, however, also speak of Antichrist as a sea-demon.) In the Christian version, just as the Beast who is Antichrist rises out of the sea, so a second beast (Rev. 13:11), identified with the False Prophet, comes out of the earth, and causes men to receive the mark of the Beast (presumably the first) on their foreheads or their right hands. Likewise, according to Surah 27:82, 'When the Word falls on them, we shall bring forth for them out of the earth a beast that shall speak unto them.' According to commentary of Ali ibn abi-Talib on this passage, when the beast appears,

> He will carry Solomon's seal and Moses' staff. He will place the seal on the face of every believer, leaving the words 'This is a believer in truth'; and on the face of infidel, leaving the words 'This is an infidel in truth'. . . . Then the beast will raise its head, and everyone from East to West will see it, after the sun has risen from the West. When it lifts its head, repentance will no longer be accepted.

The beast of the Koran is clearly neither the Antichrist nor the False Prophet of the *Apocalypse*. Yet both the beast of the Koran and the False Prophet rise from beneath the earth, from the abode of the dead, which in many traditions stands for all that has been repressed and forgotten in the individual or collective human soul. The False Prophet perhaps symbolizes the human evil hidden in that soul, just as the first beast, the Antichrist, who rises not from the earth of the human world but from the sea of the 'collective unconscious', symbolizes the part of that soul which is open to, and controlled by, a trans-human, satanic evil, the Dragon. But the beast of the Koran would seem to stand for the totality of the collective human soul, the hidden good as well as the hidden evil—the *nafs* on every level, whether commanding, accusing, or at peace, now speaking the full truth of its nature under the compulsion of the Spirit. As also happens on the spiritual Path, where travelers 'die before they are made to die', the descent of the Word or Spirit causes all that has been concealed in the soul to rise into plain view; and when this process is complete, the possibility of individual action, and thus of individual repentance, is ended, either by physical death or by annihilation in God. In the light of the Word it is men's deeds, as measured against the staff of Moses (representing the law), and their psychic dispositions, as divined by Solomon's seal (representing his power over the

Jinn, i.e., the realm of the psyche) which testify definitively as to who is destined for the Garden and who for the Fire. The faces of both groups are sealed by the seal-ring of Solomon because, according to Islamic doctrine, 'acts are judged by their intent.'

HINDU ESCHATOLOGY:
KALKI AND CHRIST COMPARED

The Hindu scriptures known as the *Puranas* are thought by some to have been composed between the 4th and the 16th centuries AD. Traditional Hindu authorities, however, attribute them to the ancient sage Vyasa, who is also believed to have composed the *Mahabarata*, and see them as written versions of much older oral traditions, since they are in fact mentioned in the *Upanishads* (c. 600–300 BC) and even the *Brahmanas* (c. 800–600 BC). The word 'purana' itself means 'ancient', or perhaps 'ancient-new', in order to express the perennial freshness and timeliness of the primordial wisdom. There are eighteen major puranas: six dedicated to Brahma, six to Vishnu, and six to Shiva. The Vaishnava puranas contain the Hindu doctrine of cosmic cycles, as well the history of the avatars of Vishnu, of whom Krishna is probably the best-known.

The parallels between certain sections of the Puranas and the Book of *Apocalypse*, particularly parts of the *Vishnu Purana* (dated 6th century by Joseph Campbell) and the *Bhavagata Purana* (dated 10th century), are numerous and striking. These scriptures, as well as the *Bhasa Bharata* and the *Agni Purana* (which is not Vaishnava but Shaivite) contain predictions of the advent of the Kalki avatara, the 10th avatar of Vishnu in the last period of the cycle, the first nine having already come and gone. Some scholars explain this similarity on the basis of an early Christian influence within Hinduism. But it is equally likely that both renditions of the Savior destined to appear in the end-times are variations of a single tradition, related to the doctrine of the cosmic cycle or Great Year common to the ancient Mesopotamians, the Hindus, the Greeks, the Norse, and even the Lakota Sioux, and probably based on the astronomical precession of the equinoxes. Joseph Campbell traces this tradition to at least c.300 BC in Mesopotamia, though the lists of antediluvian kings numerologically related to the Great Year go back to much earlier times, while the number-system they employ, based on the number 60, is found as far back as c. 3200 BC. Sumerian and Babylonian king-lists usually name ten kings, which is also the number of patriarchs from Adam to Noah inclusively—a fact that leads one to wonder whether the Hindu doctrine of the ten major avatars of Vishnu, of which Kalki will be the last in this cycle, is a later version of the same constellation of ideas, particularly since Noah came at the end of one world-age and went on to inaugurate the next. The number ten is related to the Hindu cosmic cycle, the *manvantara*, through its division into the four *yugas*: the Satya-yuga, the Treta-yuga, the Dvapara-yuga and the Kali-yuga. The Treta-yuga is three-fourths as long as the Satya-yuga, the Dvapara-yuga one half as long, and the Kali-yuga one-fourth as long, yielding the numbers 4, 3, 2, and 1, whose sum is ten.

According to the *Vishnu Purana*,

When the practices taught by the Vedas and the institutes of the law shall have ceased, and the close of the Kali age shall be nigh, a portion of that divine being who exists of his own spiritual nature in the character of Brahma, and who is the beginning and end, and who comprehends all things, shall descend upon earth: he will be born in the family of Vishnuyasas, an eminent Brahman of Shambhala village as Kalki, endowed with the eight superhuman faculties. By his superhuman might he shall destroy all the Mlechchas [foreign barbarians] and thieves, and all whose minds are devoted to iniquity. He will then re-establish righteousness on earth; and the minds of those who live at the end of the Kali age shall be pellucid as crystal. The men who are thus changed by virtue of that particular time shall be as the seed of human beings, and shall give birth to a race who shall follow the laws of the Krita age, or age of purity [another name for the Satya-yuga].

Kalki, as 'a portion of that divine being who exists . . . as Brahma [the Creator]' is obviously analogous, though not theologically equivalent, to Christ, the Son of God the Father. He is called 'the beginning and the end', which is precisely how Christ describes himself in Rev. 1:8. His re-establishment of righteousness on earth is like the new heaven and the new earth of chapter 21 of that book, and the minds 'pellucid as crystal' of those who live to see him suggest the Heavenly Jerusalem, whose 'light was like a stone most precious, even like a jasper stone, clear as crystal' (Rev. 21:11).

The height of the wall surrounding the Heavenly Jerusalem, measured by the angel in Rev. 21:17, is given as 'an hundred forty-four cubits, the measure of a man, that is, of the angel.' This is a direct reference to the '144,000 redeemed from the earth' (Rev. 14:3), and indicates that the Heavenly Jerusalem is a projection of the 'angelic' essence of human form within the mind of God; the 144,000 redeemed are, as it were, the living bricks of that City. The 144,000, as well as the '24 elders' of Rev. 4:4,10, suggest not so much a numerical collection of individuals as a deployment, on different planes of manifestation, of the human archetype, the *seed of Man*. (In Mark 4:16, human individuals themselves are compared to seeds.) 'The men who are thus changed by virtue of that particular time' who 'shall be the seed of human beings' are thus roughly analogous to the 24 elders and the 144,000 redeemed, as long as we understand 'seed' to refer to the subtle-plane prototype of the humanity of the next aeon, the new heaven and the new earth, not to the scattered survivors of a material catastrophe. And the idea that men shall be 'changed' clearly echoes 1Cor. 15:51–52, where St Paul says 'we shall all be changed, in a moment, in the twinkling of an eye, at the last trump.'

The following is account of Kalki from the *Bhagavata Purana*:

When the Kali age, whose career is so severe to the people, is well-nigh past, the Lord will appear in his divine form (consisting of Sattva alone).... Lord Vishnu, the adored of the whole animate and inanimate creation, and the Soul of the universe, appears (in this world of matter) for protecting the virtue of the righteous and wiping out (the entire stock of) their Karma (and thereby liberating them). The Lord will appear under the name of Kalki in the house of the high-souled Vishnuyasa—the foremost Brahman of the village of Shambhala. Riding a fleet horse named

Devadutta . . . and capable of subduing the wicked, the Lord of the universe, wielding . . . the eight divine powers . . . and possessed of [endless] virtues and matchless splendor, will traverse the globe on that swift horse and exterminate with His sword in tens of millions robbers wearing the insignia of royalty. Now when all the robbers are thus exterminated, the minds of the people of the cities and the countryside will become pure indeed because of their enjoying the breezes wafting the most sacred fragrance of pigments on the person of the Lord Vasudeva [Kalki]. With Lord Vasudeva, the embodiment of strength, in their heart their progeny will grow exceedingly strong. . . . When the Lord Sri Hari, the Protector of Dharma, appears as Kalki, Satyayuga [the Golden Age] will prevail (once more). . . .

Martin Lings, in *The Eleventh Hour*, identifies Kalki with both Maitreya Buddha and the Christ:

Like Christianity, [Hinduism] depends on the *Avatara*, that is, the descent of Divinity into this world; and for the maintenance of the tradition there is a succession of no less than ten Avataras. As far as historic times are concerned, the seventh and eighth of these, Rama and Krishna, are the most important for Hinduism itself. The ninth, specifically non-Hindu (literally 'foreign') is generally considered to be the Buddha; and the tenth, Kalki, 'the rider on the white horse', will have the universal function of closing this cycle of time and inaugurating the next, which identified his descent with the second advent of Christ.

The 'rider on the white horse' appears in the same role as Kalki in the 19th chapter of Revelation:

And I saw heaven opened, and behold a white horse; and he that sat upon him was called Faithful and True, and in righteousness he doth judge and make war.

And his eyes were as a flame of fire, and on his head were many crowns; and he had a name written, that no man knew, but he himself. (19:11–12)

And out of his mouth goeth a sharp sword, that with it he should smite the nations: and he shall rule them with a rod of iron: and he treadeth the winepress of the fierceness and wrath of Almighty God. (19:15)

And I saw the beast, and the kings of the earth, and their armies (i.e., the 'tens of millions' [of] robbers wearing the insignia of royalty) gathered together to make war against him that sat on the horse, and against his army. And the beast was taken, and with him the false prophet that wrought miracles before him, with which he deceived them that had received the mark of the beast, and them that worshipped his image. These both were cast alive into a lake of fire burning with brimstone. And the remnant were slain with the sword of him that sat upon the horse, which proceeded out of his mouth: and all the fowls were filled with their flesh. (19:19–21)

In Eastern Orthodox icons, both St Michael and St George are shown riding on white horses, doing battle with the Antichrist and the Dragon respectively. The striking similarities between Hindu and Christian eschatology can be explained, I suppose, by a diffusion of motifs. Yet as a friend of mine pointed out, no integral tradition accepts myths or doctrines from outside its borders unless they are intrinsically compatible with its central vision. Hinduism and Christianity, when they look toward the end of the Aeon, gaze deeply upon the same objective reality. Nor is this visionary disclosure of the spiritual archetypes incompatible with any particular stream of historical influence, because history is providential; the eternal, spiritual world is the ultimate source of the historical one: 'time is the moving image of Eternity.'

HINDU, JUDEO-CHRISTIAN, LAKOTA, AND HOPI ESCHATOLOGY COMPARED

As I have already pointed out, one of the greatest errors of the New Age, which has infiltrated liberal Christianity as well, is to identify the primal religions with their own anti-transcendentalism, to implicitly deny nature as a theophany of the Great Spirit and take it instead as a material object—'Spaceship Earth'—to be worshipped in and for itself. However, those of the primal religions which have preserved the Primordial Tradition relatively intact have a much greater affinity with the great revealed religions than with contemporary Neo-Paganism or New Age ideology. Evidence of this

affinity can be seen in many areas of myth and doctrine, and one of these is eschatology. Both Lakota and Hindu traditions, for example, share the doctrine of a continuous cycle-of-manifestation, each cycle divided into four ages. I quote from Traditionalist author Joseph Epes Brown:

> Accounting to Siouan [Lakota] mythology, it is believed that at the beginning of the cycle a buffalo was placed at the West in order to hold back the waters. Every year this buffalo loses one hair, and every age he loses one leg. When all his hair and all four legs are gone, then the waters rush in again, and the cycle comes to an end.

> A striking parallel to this myth is found in the Hindu tradition, where it is the bull Dharma (the divine law) who has four legs, each of which represents an age of the total cycle. During the course of these four ages (*yugas*), true spirituality becomes increasingly obscured, until the cycle (*manvantara*) closes with a catastrophe, after which the primordial spirituality is restored, and the cycle begins once again.

> It is believed by both the American Indian and the Hindu that at the present time the buffalo or bull is on his last leg, and he is very nearly bald. Corresponding beliefs could be cited from many other traditions. See René Guénon, *The Crisis of the Modern World.*[6]

As for parallels with Judeo-Christian eschatology, perhaps the clearest is the Lakota doctrine of the sacred 'red and blue days'. 'These,'

---

6. *The Sacred Pipe: Black Elk's Account of the Seven Rites of the Oglala Sioux*, p9, n15. See also Frithjof Schuon, *The Feathered Sun* (Bloomington, IN: World Wisdom Books, 1990), pp113–114.

according to Joseph Epes Brown, 'are the days at the end of the world when the moon will turn red and the sun will turn blue. But, since for the traditional man everything in the macrocosm has its counterpart in the microcosm, there may be an end of the world for the individual here and now, whenever he receives illumination from *Wakan-Tanka,* so that his ego or ignorance dies, and then he lives continually in the Spirit.'

According to the prophet Joel (2:31, echoed in Matt. 24:29 and Mark 13:24), 'The sun shall be turned into darkness, and the moon into blood, before the great and terrible day of the Lord.' Both traditions state that the moon will turn red, and the sun is certainly 'darkened' if it turns blue. Furthermore, dark blue is identified with or substituted for black in the color symbolism of many nations. Blue-skinned Krishna is sometimes called *Kala,* 'the black one', and in Richard Wilhelm's commentary on his translation of the *I Ching* it is stated that 'Black, or rather dark blue, is the color of heaven.' According to Epes Brown, blue (not surprisingly) is also 'the color of the heavens' in Lakota symbolism.

The darkened sun and red moon obviously relate to solar and lunar eclipses; a moon in eclipse will often show a dull red color. But few seem to know that the actual color of the midday sun to the naked eye, as I proved to myself during childhood by staring into it for short periods, is a shimmering blue-black. As for the symbolic meanings of these colors as attributed to sun and moon, they can be taken on at least two levels. From the point of view of the 'ego or ignorance' as it dies, the darkening of the sun represents the veiling of the Intellect, as when Jesus on the cross cried out, 'My God, my God, why have you forsaken me?' and the reddening of the moon the outbreak of the passions. When the Intellect is veiled, the passions run riot; such are the conditions universally predicted for the end of the Kali-yuga. The moon is a universal symbol for the world of the psyche, which is turned both toward the 'sublunar' cycles of nature as their proximate cause, and toward the Sun of the Intellect, its ultimate Source. The second orientation is the symbolic meaning of the moon in Islam, representing not so much the psyche in itself as the transcendent center of the psyche, the 'Heart'—the level of being the Virgin Mary was speaking from in Mark 1:46 when she said 'My soul doth magnify the Lord.' The first orientation is represented by the various pagan moon-goddesses who rule the cycles of fertility.

From the point of view of the eternal archetypes, however, blue sun and red moon have a different meaning. As we have seen, René Guénon in *The Reign of Quantity* presents the course of any cycle of manifestation as a descent from the pole of Essence, whose symbol is the sun, to the pole of Substance, symbolized by the moon. But Essence and Substance, as archetypes, never themselves enter into manifestation, the first because of its exaltation, the second because of its simplicity. Just as Essence is above form, and therefore inconceivable, so Substance is below form, and consequently incapable of being discovered or possessed (this, incidentally, is why the quest of physics for an 'ultimate particle', or its equivalent, will never end).

Insofar as Essence and Substance are echoed in the manifest world, Essence appears (in Aristotelian terms) as *forma* or prototype, that which confers form, and Substance as matrix or *materia*, that which receives form. As the cycle descends, however, *forma* gradually becomes obscured behind the veils of *materia*, while *materia* progressively adopts the prerogatives of *forma*, though only in an illusory sense; as the eternal forms through which God creates the material world become hidden, it begins to seem as if matter somehow had the power to create itself. The celestial blue of *forma* is darkened, while *materia* takes on the angry red hue of self-assertive materialism; in the words of Charles Peguy (which epitomize, in a sense, the doctrine of world-ages from Plato's *Republic*): 'everything begins in mysticism and ends in politics.' *Forma* and *materia* ultimately become so confused with one another that the world-sustaining polarity between them breaks down, and the cycle ends in chaos. But when the sun turns blue and the moon turns red, this indicates a purifying re-polarization of forma and *materia*, which returns them to their original archetypes. The blue sun is a symbol of Essence or pure quality manifesting as the celestial order, the Father principle; the red moon is a symbol of Substance or pure receptivity manifesting as life energy, the power to draw essences or qualities into manifestation, the Mother principle. *Forma* is no longer encumbered now by the dark shells of *materia*, but directly reveals Essence, while *materia* no longer arrogates to itself the power to confer form, but directly manifests the receptive virginity of Substance. So the stage is set for the reunion of Divine Father and Divine Mother, the 'wedding feast of the Lamb', the procreation of 'a new heaven and a new earth'.

Joseph Epes Brown presents the Lakota doctrine of *forma* vs. Essence and *materia* vs. Substance as follows:

> As the distinction is made within Wakan-Tanka between Father and Grandfather, so the Earth is considered under two aspects, that of Mother and Grandmother. The former is the earth considered as the producer of all growing forms, in act; whereas Grandmother refers to the ground or substance of all growing things—potentiality. This distinction is the same as that made by the Christian Scholastics between *natura naturans* and *natura naturata*. (p6, n7)

Mother Earth, then, is *materia,* and Grandmother Earth is Substance; Father and Grandfather Spirit are *forma* and Essence; or, on a higher octave, Being and Beyond-being. According to Epes Brown,

> *Wakan-Tanka* as Grandfather is the Great Spirit independent of manifestation, unqualified, unlimited, identical to the Christian Godhead, or to the Hindu *Brahma-Nirguna*. *Wakan-Tanka* as Father is the Great Spirit considered in relation to His manifestation, either as Creator, Preserver, or Destroyer, identical to the Christian God, or the Hindu *Brahma-Saguna*. (p5, n6)

The Hopi, too, have a tradition of four successive worlds, which are both temporal ages and ontological levels. According to *The Book of the Hopi* by Frank Waters, the first world is Tokpela, Endless Space. On one level, Tokpela is the world of Beyond Being, where Tiowa, the Formless Absolute,

exists in solitude, before creation; on another, it is the world of the first creation. (As the four ages progress, they become less like ontological levels and more like historical periods; we are moving from the pole of qualitative *forma* to that of quantitative *materia*). In this guise, since it is associated with the mineral *sikyasvu*, gold, it is obviously the Golden Age. In Tokpela—perhaps to be identified with the paleolithic—the people live in peace with the animals and with each other. It is destroyed partly through the deceptions of Kato'ya, the handsome one, who is described as 'a snake with a big head', clearly analogous to the serpent in *Genesis*. (This is interesting, given that the Hopi are among the tribes least influenced by Christianity.) As the first world begins to degenerate, the chosen from among the people begin their migration; they follow a cloud by day and a star by night, just as the chosen people in *Exodus* follow a pillar of cloud and a pillar of fire. As Tokpela is destroyed by fire, they take refuge underground with the Ant People, who are analogous to the primordial earth-born ant-men of Greek myth, the *myrmidons*.

Next the people emerge from the underground world of the ants and enter the second world, Tokpa, Dark Midnight, whose mineral is *qochasiva*, silver. This is the Silver Age, apparently the neolithic, when handicrafts and village life are developed. The second world is destroyed by water and ice when the twins Poqanghoya and Palongawhoya, guardians of the poles, leave their stations and the earth flips over twice. The people again take refuge underground with the ants, and then emerge into the third world.

The third world, Kuskurza, is related to the mineral *palasiva*, copper—a major constituent of bronze. So we are now in the Bronze Age. In Kuskurza the people overpopulate and use their reproductive power for evil—copper being identified, in traditional symbolism, with Venus, the erotic principle. They develop a high technology, live in cities, and fly on shields covered with hide called *patuwvotas*—strikingly similar to the flying *vimanas* described in the Hindu *puranas*—which they use as engines of war. Kuskurza, like Atlantis, is destroyed by water; whole continents sink beneath the waves.

As the third world is about to end, Spider Woman—a figure who is something like the *shekhinah* of Sotuknang, the demiurge, the first created being, who in turn is the active energy of Tiowa, the Creator—tells the people to get inside of hollow reeds to escape from the flood. She later directs them to make these reeds into boats. She leads them in a migration over water, searching for the fourth world. (The boats made of reeds remind one of the Egyptian reed boat that Thor Heyerdahl used to cross the Atlantic in his Ra Expedition, thus proving that the Egyptians—or Atlanteans—could have populated the New World, though the direction of their journey, East and a little North, suggests a Southwest Asian origin.) During this migration, they send out birds for land, just as Noah did in *Genesis*, but no land is to be found.

After stopping at a continent which was not their true destination, they arrive at the fourth world, called Tuwaqachi, the World Complete, where life is hard. This is the world we presently occupy. The mineral associated with the fourth world is the 'mixed mineral' *sikyapala*, analogous to the iron mixed with clay which composes the feet of the statue dreamt of by King Nebuchadnezzar in the Book of Daniel; so Tuwaqachi would seem to be the Iron Age. The spiritual guardian of Tuwaqachi is Masaw, who was also the ruler of Kuskurza, the third world, and who brought it to an end through his corruption. He is here because Tiowa decided to give him a second chance—a chance he seems to have wasted. The Hopi myth clearly implies that this world too will be destroyed by the abuse of reproductive power and high technology. Here we can see again, through the convergence of Hinduism, Judeo-Christianity, Aristotle and the teachings of the Hopi and the Lakota Sioux, how traditional metaphysics, the science of eternal principles, is both primordial and universal.

THE SIEGE OF SHAMBHALA:
TIBETAN BUDDHIST ESCHATOLOGY

Tibetan Buddhist eschatology, notably the lore which appears in the Kalachakra Tantra, differs in important respects from that of other forms of Buddhism. In *Tibet* by Thubten Jigme Norbu (Simon & Schuster, 1968), a tulku of the Gelugpa Lineage and elder brother of the Dalai Lama, the following account is given, which has clear affinities with the eschatologies of many other traditions. The *Shambhala Smonlam* says:

> Fearless, in the midst of your army of gods,
> Among your twelve divisions,
> You ride on horseback.
> You thrust your spear toward the chest of Hanumanda,
> Minister of the evil forces drawn up
> Against Shambhala.
> So shall evil be destroyed.

Shambhala is the name of a city and country 'to the North' where some of the original teachings of Tibetan Tantra are believed to have originated. In the final period of the cycle, when religion and morality will have degenerated and the earth grown colder, the city of Shambhala will be the only place on earth where the teachings of Buddha are preserved. As soon as the encroaching corruption of the surrounding world reaches the city walls, the god-king of Shambhala will ride out against the leader of the evil forces and slay him.

Lhasa will be covered with water during that time. After evil is destroyed, Tsong Khapa will arise from his tomb at the Ganden Monastery and Buddhism will be renewed for a thousand years. Then will come the end of the world, which will be accomplished first by fire, then by wind, then by water. A very few human beings will survive, in treetops and caves (esoterically speaking, by virtue of intellectual height and spiritual depth). The gods will come from Ganden Paradise and take these people back with them, who will receive spiritual teachings and become immortal. Finally, when the wind again churns the milky ocean and the world is re-created, those enlightened ones of the final days, saved from the former cycle of manifestation, will be the stars in the sky. (Compare Dan. 12:3, according to which, at the end of time, 'they that be wise shall shine as the brightness of the firmament; and they that turn many to righteousness as the stars for ever and ever.')

Hanumanda would appear to be something like a Tibetan Antichrist. (Elsewhere his name is given as Krinmati, a barbarian overlord.) The twelve divisions of his opponent the god-king are paralleled by the '[more than] twelve legions of angels' ready to defend Jesus in Matt. 26:53, as well as the 12,000 followers of Ali who rise from the dead at the coming of the Mahdi in Muslim eschatology, and the 12,000 sealed elect from each of the 12 tribes of Israel in Rev. 7:4–8. (The number 12 obviously suggests the Zodiac, which would identify the various eschatological armies with what are called in the Old Testament 'the host of heaven'—the stars: 'The stars in their courses are fighting on the side of the just.') The siege of Shambhala itself clearly suggests the battle of Armageddon, when Jerusalem will be encompassed by armies. 'I will gather all nations against Jerusalem to battle; and the city shall be taken. . . . Then shall the Lord go forth, and fight against those nations. . . .' (Zech. 14:2–3). The motif of the 'rapture' also appears, as found in both Christian and Islamic tradition, along with the myth of the millennium—Tibetan Buddhist eschatology, according to the present rendition, is 'pre-millennialist'—as well as the prophecy that the mounted eschatological hero will slay an Antichrist-like figure with a spear or lance.

According to the account given by John Newman, co-author of *The Wheel of Time: Kalachakra in Context* (Madison: Deer Park Books, 1985), the 'messiah' figure and king of Shambhala who defeats the forces of evil is Raudra Charki—who, interestingly enough, is named as the last of the 'Kalkis', a lineage of the rulers of Shambhala founded by the first Kalki, the great Yashas, whose queen was Tara. So he would seem to be at least partly identifiable with the Kalki Avatara of the Hindu *Puranas*. Raudra Charki's grandson, future ruler of Shambhala, will be Kashyapa, the name given to Maitreya's herald in the Mahayana prophecy recounted above.

The fact that the earth will be colder during the Siege of Shambhala suggests the Norse *Fimbulwinter*, as well as elements in the Zoroastrian myth of the Var of Yima (see below), of which the legend of Shambhala appears to be a Tibetan rendition. Both Shambhala and the Var of Yima are situated 'in the North', making them variations on the theme of the Hyperborean Paradise.

According to some Tibetan accounts, the city of Shambhala is near the Oxus river in Central Asia. This would seem to confirm the tradition repeated by Gurdjieff follower J.G. Bennett that the word Shambhala, according to folk-etymology at least, is really the Arabic Shams-i-Balkh, 'Sun of Balkh', the name of the Zoroastrian

Fire-temple in the ancient city of Balkh in the valley of the Oxus. In an alternate and possibly more reliable account given by John Newman, however, Shambhala is located in the Tarim basin, directly to the north of Tibet, east and slightly to the north of Balkh. Newman identifies the Sita river mentioned in the Kalachakra scriptures with the Tarim. In the *Vishnu Purana* on the other hand, Shambhala is the small village in India where the Kalki Avatara will be born. But wherever the quasi-geographical Shambhala may or may not be located, the true site of this miraculous city-state is in the 'Eighth Clime', the *alam al-mithal*, the Imaginal Plane. Its god-king, the Kalki, is—like King Arthur, the immortal prophets Khidr and Elijah, the Zoroastrian Yima, and the occulted Twelfth Imam—one more rendition of Guénon's 'King of the World', the archetype of Man for the present aeon, enthroned on the subtle plane, and surrounded by the Terrestrial Paradise, which is his emanation, his *shakti*.

The eschatological lore of many traditions is reflected in the mirror of this Tibetan 'legend of the end'.

BENJAMIN CREME:
PROPHET OF THE THEOSOPHICAL ANTICHRIST

All quotes are taken from *The Emergence Quarterly,* background information issue, a free publication of the Maitreya Movement

As a counterpoint to these traditional eschatologies, we should take some time to look at one of the clearest of the contemporary inverted eschatologies, that of Benjamin Creme, whose teachings are based on the doctrines of the Theosophical Society, particularly those of Alice Bailey, author of *The Reappearance of Christ* (1948). Creme is so obviously playing the role of False Prophet to his occulted 'Maitreya' figure as Antichrist, that one suspects he may be doing it deliberately. His 'Antichrist' is probably too literal a false Messiah to be the real Antichrist; still, Creme's ministry demonstrates how the roles of 'Antichrist' and 'False Prophet' are in the air right now.

Creme claims to be in constant telepathic contact with the 'Master Maitreya', who is the one expected by Christians as Jesus, by Jews as the Messiah, by Muslims as the Mahdi, etc. 'Maitreya' descended from his mountain retreat in the Himalayas in 1977 to become an Indian or Pakistani living in London. He comes not as a religious leader but as a guide to those of all religions, as well as atheists. 'A real disciple', he says, 'is one who will respect the traditions. Respect your own religions, your own ideologies—in brief, your own thought-form, and you will experience the Master.' Clearly the truth of religion, or of the secular ideologies, does not concern him. It doesn't even matter whether or not you believe in God. 'Maitreya' gives lip service to the transcendent unity of traditional religious doctrines; his teachings, however, repeatedly contradict these doctrines. The Master is apparently 'above' questions of truth, and it is for this reason that I do not believe what he says. Under the influence of his energy, says Creme, 'more and more people will revolt, because old habits, centuries-old codes imposed on the mind, must be broken. People will not accept imposed solutions.' This does not sound, to me, much like respect for all traditions and ideologies.

Commercialization and the reign of market forces are a scourge, says 'Maitreya'. I agree. 'The new politics will no longer be molded by the 'isms' of capitalism or socialism, but created from self-respect in individuals and nations. Liberty, freedom and salvation will be the objectives of everyone', Creme writes, 'and they are all the same. The reality of global interdependence will become an established fact in our awareness.' Well, it has. But today's new sense of global interdependence, which is becoming increasingly burdensome and anxiety-ridden, is precisely a product of commercialization and market forces. And if both the hard lessons of history and an elemental understanding of psychology haven't yet taught us that freedom and salvation are not always the same thing, then there's little I can add. External freedom sometimes serves salvation and sometimes undermines it, but no one who is not willing, if need be, to sacrifice self-determined action in order to save his soul, has yet learned the difference between the bondage of libertinism and the Liberation which can only come from strict obedience to the Source of love and truth. Such obedience is, however, foreign to

Creme. 'The politicians alone, Maitreya says, are to blame for the desperation of those addicted to drugs. 'If people are so straitened in life that they cannot even eat properly ... they will lead desperate lives.' This is a half-truth, obviously: are there no such things as rich drug addicts?

Creme banks on a world economic crash starting in Japan to bring us to our senses, awaken us to higher values, and give 'Maitreya' a chance to take over. He apparently hopes for a Theosophical world revolution of the 2000s on the order of the Communist upsurgence during the Great Depression of the 1930s.

It was 'Maitreya' who decreed the fall of the Soviet Union and ended Apartheid in South Africa. It is he who is presently producing, from somewhere in the London suburbs, all the apparitions of angels, the Virgin Mary, the Buddha and Christ throughout the world, miraculous healing wells, milk-drinking statues in India, vanishing hitchhikers predicting the Second Coming, and mysterious crosses of light appearing in windows all over the world, starting in southern California. His 'platform' is simple: The unity of humanity; a new civilization based on sharing, economic and social justice and global cooperation; adequate food, clothing, housing, and medical care; the regeneration of the environment; and an end to world hunger, along with mass spiritual enlightenment: a Buddha in every pot. As Dennis Engleman writes in *Ultimate Things* (pp179–180),

> Antichrist will develop a reputation as a phenomenal problem-solver. His uncanny ability to anticipate outcomes and to propose solutions will seem prophetic and visionary to a world unaware of his secret manipulations. War, economic disturbance, social injustice, political instability, religious intolerance—no difficulty will escape his soothing touch.

Who can disagree with these lofty goals? Who but the superstitious, the hide-bound, the corrupt or the insane could oppose them? Who but degenerates, said Hitler, could oppose full employment, a more spiritual culture which gives hope and direction to the young, and an end to the shameful and oppressive provisions of the Treaty of Versailles? Who but bourgeois reactionaries, said Marx, could oppose a classless society, based on the principle of 'from each according to his abilities, to each according to his needs', where no one over-indulges and no one starves? What 'Maitreya' proposes is good—but good, of course, can be co-opted. And what can be expected from someone who claims to be engineering massive world changes, as well as a global manifestation of vanishing hitch-hikers, from somewhere in the London suburbs? Or from people imbalanced enough to believe in him?

A recurrent theme in 'Maitreya's' teachings, like those of the founder of EST, the late Werner Erhardt, is the ending of world hunger. What could be more compassionate, more blameless? However, according to Sachedina in *Islamic Messianism*, p173,

> Al-Dajjal's [the Antichrist's] role at the End of Time is almost identical to that of Satan, as explained in traditional sources, because he will tempt people by bringing food and water, which will be scarce at that time.

Creme looks forward to the day when 'Maitreya' will manifest himself to the world:

> At the earliest possible moment, Maitreya will demonstrate His true identity. On the Day of Declaration, the international television networks will be linked together. By invitation of the media, we will see Maitreya's face on television, but He will not speak. Instead, each of us will hear his words telepathically in our own language as he simultaneously impresses the minds of all humanity. Even those who are not watching Him on television will have this experience. At the same time, hundreds of thousands of spontaneous healings will take place throughout the world. In this way we will know that this man is truly the World Teacher for all humanity.

So Creme and his Theosophical friends are hoping to stage a global mass- suggestion event. According to *Ultimate Things* (pp134–135),

> A mankind accustomed to laser shows, high-definition television and other spectacles will be thrilled by Antichrist. The media will love him; public figures of all types will turn out in his support.

Yet the enthusiasm will have sinister origins. Saint Ignatius Brianchaninov warns, 'The false spirits, sent throughout the world, will incite in men a generally high opinion of the antichrist, universal ecstasy, irresistible attraction to him.' As John the Baptist, 'the Forerunner', prepared the way for Jesus' public ministry, a uniquely cunning man will set the stage for Antichrist's advent. This person, referred to in Scripture as 'the false prophet', will enthrall the world by means of cunningly staged spectacles.... A humanity taught by science that whatever they want they can have, and by Hollywood to believe that whatever they see is true, will be enchanted and mystified by the wonders of the false prophet. His magical presentations will pique, and at the same time deaden, the longing in their souls for true heavenly visions. (pp 182–183)

In the words of Martin Lings,

As in Christianity, it is believed in Islam that [the Antichrist] will cause corruption, and that by his power to work marvels he will win many to his side.[7]

According to Creme, 'Maitreya' has been emerging *gradually* into the public view so as not to infringe humanity's free will.' But according to Engleman (p 254),

Unlike Antichrist, who will have had to deceive mankind, and use all the modern technology available to advance his cause, Christ's Second Advent will cause an immediate spiritual shock throughout the world. 'It will not be necessary or possible for persons to communicate news of the coming of the Son of God', wrote Saint Ignatius Brianchaninov. 'He will appear suddenly ... to all men and to all the earth at the same time.'

I won't go into Creme's 'esoteric philosophy' in detail, since it is basically that of the Theosophical Society. I will, however, quote three passages. The first is attributed to the master Djwhal Khul, as channeled by Alice Bailey: 'All activity which drives the human

7. *The Eleventh Hour*, pp 97–99.

being forward toward some form of development—physical, emotional, intuitional, social—if it is in advance of his present state, is essentially spiritual in nature.' But 'in advance' toward what? The thug working out so as to be a stronger thug, the thief sharpening his senses and manual dexterity so as to be a better thief, the spy developing his intuition so as to be a better spy—these are spiritual pursuits? (According to the way my own intuition has developed, I hear in the name 'Djwhal Khul' the Arabic words *Dajjal*, 'Antichrist', and *Qul*, 'recite'.)

The second passage attempts to define the nature of God: 'Esotericism postulates that *God* is the sum total of all the laws, and all the energies governed by these laws, which make up everything in the manifested and unmanifested universe—all that we see and cannot see.' This is not esotericism, however, but scientism, the familiar superstitious worship of natural laws and invisible energies which always crops up when theology is influenced by science, or when popularized science is turned into a religion. True esoterism, on the other hand, knows God as an Absolute, Perfect and Infinite Essence Who is equally a Person, a Reality which in Itself cannot be grasped or encompassed in terms of any conceivable form. God is inconceivable not because He is devoid of personhood, but because, rather than being this or that person, He is Personhood Itself—not as an abstract category, however, but as a unique Essence. For the vulgar and muddled 'esotericism' of Benjamin Creme, on the other hand, God is nothing but a heap of everything, an infinite conglomeration of every this and every that.

The third passage is of more immediate interest:

According to the Ageless Wisdom, the *anti-Christ* is not one individual who lives at a certain point in time, but an *energy* released before the advent of the Christ. It comes to pave the way for the building-forces of the Christ by destroying the old crystallized ways that block growth for society. While the anti-Christ is an energy, it does manifest through individuals and has done so at different times throughout history, most notably through the Emperor Nero in Roman times, and more recently through Hitler and some of his closest associates. With the defeat

COMPARATIVE ESCHATOLOGY 69

of the Axis powers during World War II, the work of the anti-Christ energy was completed for this age and will not manifest again for over 3,000 years.

So if Benjamin Creme is to be believed—as clearly he wants to be, and with very good reason—'Master Maitreya' cannot be the Antichrist! But *Hitler*, pave the way for the Christ? Hitler as John the Baptist, as Elijah? I don't think so. In the words of Orthodox Archbishop Averky of Jordanville, as recounted in *Ultimate Things*,

> The fundamental task of the servants of the coming Antichrist is to destroy the old world with all its former concepts and 'prejudices' in order to build in its place a new world suitable for receiving its approaching 'new owner' who will take the place of Christ for people and give them on earth that which Christ did not give them.

We must never forget that what appears as ridiculous on the surface may be profoundly sinister in its depths; as 'Master Maitreya' himself tells us, complacency is among the worst of vices. Dr Rama Coomaraswamy, in his essay 'The Desacralization of Hinduism for Western Consumption', has this to say regarding Alice Bailey, who succeeded Annie Besant as head of the Theosophical Society, and her plans for a new world religion:

> It is interesting to look at Bailey's instructions about the orthodox religions of the world. Initially the New Agers are to argue for religious liberty in their public releases. Only later will they insist on the new mandatory world religion that their books call for, a religion completely breaking with the concept of Jesus Christ and God the Father. Those who do not go along with this are to be eliminated by means of violence—called by her 'a cleansing action'. We are clearly on the way to point Omega and the reign of antichrist.

MOTIF OF THE HERALD:
THE WILL AND THE INTELLECT

In most eschatological traditions, the coming Messiah or Avatar is heralded by a forerunner, as Jesus by John the Baptist. In Jewish eschatology, the Messiah is to be announced by Elias, one of the two prophets of the Old Testament who never suffered death, which is why the contemporaries of Jesus wondered if John the Baptist might be Elias come back. The second coming of Jesus is to be announced by the 'two witnesses' of the Apocalypse, who are identified with Elias and Enoch, the second of the two immortal prophets of the Old Testament. The advent of the Buddha Maitreya will be heralded by Shakyamuni's disciple Kashyapa, who has also remained in some form of 'occultation' or suspended animation, and that of Saoshyant by Keresaspa, who will likewise remain immortal on the plane of subtle manifestation until his time arrives. The descent of the Prophet Jesus in Islamic eschatology will be announced by the Mahdi, who has survived through the ages in suspended animation or 'occultation', just as the Mahdi himself, in the Shiïte account, is heralded by the 'voice from the east after sunrise.' And though the Kalki Avatara is not announced by a specific figure, he is 'hosted' by Vishnuyasa the Brahmin, in whose household he is born, just as Maitreya is born in the same household as King Dhutta-Gamani, his brother, or during the reign of King Shanka. (The resurrection of the great Tibetan teacher Tsong Khapa, whose name certainly sounds like 'Kashyapa' and 'Keresaspa', is a similar motif, though Tsong Khapa is not a herald.)

So the eschatological Savior almost always has a partner, who usually arrives before him to announce his coming. The announcer has remained in suspended animation over the long ages, while the Savior, though in a sense representing the re-appearance of an earlier Savior, also carries the flavor of an entirely new advent, a descent of Eternity into time, a re-manifestation of saving Truth, fresh from the celestial worlds. (In the Zoroastrian account it is Yima the first prophet who remains in suspended animation, to return at the advent of Saoshyant.)

The relationship between the Savior and his herald is also that between a partial and a complete manifestation of the same reality. John the Baptist was a militant prophet, Jesus a priest and king. The same is true of Elias vis- à-vis the Messiah, or the defeated Messiah son of Joseph vs. the triumphant Messiah son of David. In Islam the Mahdi is the herald of the prophet Jesus, since he comes before him. However, Jesus will worship behind al-Mahdi, who will act as Imam (in the sense of prayer-leader), though this is perhaps best understood as an act of supreme courtesy, since al-Mahdi will initially seek to yield his place to Jesus. And according to al-Jili's account, Jesus is the militant one, since he slays Antichrist, while the Mahdi who dawns after the battle is done personifies equilibrium restored. The Buddha Maitreya, who is a *brahmin*, in some accounts is announced by his brother and first disciple, King Dhutta-Gamani, rather than by Kashyapa, just as the herald and first disciple of Jesus was his cousin, John the Baptist; according to other versions, Maitreya is destined to appear and work with the universal monarch Shanka. In Hindu eschatological tradition, the militant Kalki Avatara is born in the household of the *brahmin* Vishnuyasa.

In every case, then, we have an eschatological partnership between a militant figure and a 'spiritual' or pneumatic one. The polarization of the Jewish Messiah into priestly and kingly versions (to take only one example) is thus a universal motif. This can be explained historically as a product of the tension between the repeated failure of Messianic hopes in their political expression and the eternal hope for spiritual renewal; political defeat always forces the defeated to ask how their intent might have been purer and their dedication deeper, and such questioning often leads to the idea that only after the people have spiritually purified themselves will salvation come. This is why revolutionary messianism is often pre-millennialist, and spiritual messianism (insofar as it grows out of revolutionary defeat) post-millennialist. But since history itself is the fluid expression in time of eternal metaphysical principles, the roots of the polarization between militant and pneumatic eschatological figures must be sought on higher planes of being.

In some cases the militant is the herald and the pneumatic the Savior; in others the reverse is true. The Christ of the first advent (announced by John), the Buddhist Maitreya (announced by Dhutta-Gamani) and the Mahdi vis-à-vis Jesus (at least in al-Jili's account) are spirituals announced or preceded by militants. On the other hand, the Jewish Messiah (heralded by Elias), the Kalki Avatara of Hinduism (paired with Vishnuyasa) and the Word of God in the *Apocalypse*, the Christ of the Second Coming (heralded by Enoch and Elias) are militants announced or hosted by spirituals. This characterization is far from perfect, obviously, since the Elias who announces the Messiah was certainly a prophetic militant during his earthly life, which is why many of the Jews recognized the same quality in the militant Baptist. And in the various Muslim accounts, Jesus is sometimes the militant slayer of Antichrist and al-Mahdi the restorer of equilibrium after the battle, while sometimes he is the one who, after the Mahdi himself is overcome by Antichrist, overcomes him in turn and so restores order. But the polarization between militancy and transcendence, however it is worked out in a particular tradition or account, remains in clear relief.

In my opinion, the significance of this pairing is as follows: The militant figures represent the will, the spiritual ones the Intellect. Will asserted, will defeated, and Intellect unveiled are thesis, antithesis and synthesis; the will, at least on the human level, must both do its best work and admit its ultimate powerlessness before the Intellect can dawn. At the beginning of the spiritual Path, the traveler wills to follow God, he takes full personal responsibility. Then commanding *nafs* constellates, showing the individual will its ultimate powerlessness; finally God (if He so wills) takes the field and slays the *nafs*. Moses kills the overseer, flees to the wilderness, and sees God in the burning bush. Christ ministers, is crucified, and rises. Muhammad receives his mission, is exiled to Medina, returns to Mecca in triumph. The Messiah son of Joseph is defeated by Antichrist, who in turn is overcome Messiah son of David. The Twelfth Imam appears, is occulted, returns on the Last Day.

As on the spiritual Path so in the eschatological scenario: from one perspective, a person's individual effort to grow in the Spirit precedes the full dawning of that Spirit; from another, it is the initial free gift of that Spirit which alone makes such effort possible. That Moses kills the Egyptian overseer and flees into the wilderness, after which God speaks to him, indicates in esoteric terms that the struggle of the human will against the lower self—even though that will cannot triumph in its own terms (Moses did not gain personal power through killing the overseer but became a homeless fugitive)—must still precede the dawning of the Transcendent Intellect, to which it finally makes obeisance. The same truth is symbolized in Islam by the conquest of the Antichrist by the Prophet Jesus (i.e., the overcoming of the will of the lower self by the will obedient to, and empowered by, God), and the subsequent restoration of equilibrium by the Mahdi (the dawning of the Divine Intellect after the will, in victory and defeat, is pacified), and in the Jewish one by the Messiah son of Joseph who goes to battle with the Antichrist and is killed, only to be followed by the Messiah son of David who defeats and kills the Antichrist. In Buddhist tradition, the fact that the King Shanka of the *kshatriya* or warrior caste renounces his throne to follow the *brahmin* Maitreya reflects the identical doctrine. In Schuon's words,

> What separates man from the Divine Reality is the slightest of barriers. God is infinitely close to man, but man is infinitely far from God. This barrier, for man, is a mountain ... which he must remove with his own hands. He digs away the earth, but in vain, the mountain remains; man however goes on digging in the Name of God. And the mountain vanishes. It was never there.[8]

In another sense, however, the Divine Truth, which the Intellect both sees and is, cannot be realized unless the will makes obeisance to it. So while the Intellect remains on a higher plane than the will, the full activation of the will in service of the Intellect represents the complete incarnation, or realization, of what on the plane of the Intellect is only virtual in relation to man, though complete and fully realized in relation to God. Furthermore, there is nothing more militant and rigorous in its effects than the dawning of objective Truth. Absolute objectivity, the sword of the discriminating Intellect, is both perfect judgement and perfect forgiveness, without

8. *Stations of Wisdom* (London: John Murray, 1962), p157.

the slightest distinction between them. God witnesses nothing but Himself—this is His rigor—and knows all things *as* Himself—this is His mercy.

When the immortal and occulted herald is a militant figure, this possibly represents the maintenance of a spiritual tradition on the legalistic level alone, paired with a suspension of the full power of human obedience until the direct knowledge of God is again unveiled. When the hidden herald is a pneumatic figure, this may symbolize a guardianship of esoteric lore by marginalized or clandestine schools, or such lore as preserved, unbeknownst to its preservers, in the forms of exoteric religion, until such time as inner spiritual potentials can again be manifested outwardly in the fullness of human life.

THE 'BRIEF MILLENNIUM'

Those writers of the Traditionalist school who deal most directly with eschatology—René Guénon, Martin Lings, and Leo Schaya—do not anticipate an earthly millennium of the latter days. They are not chiliasts. They do, however, see a brief 'restoration' before the end of the cycle. In *Perspectives on Initiation* (p254), René Guénon has this to say about the advent of the Mahdi:

Moreover, this [total Messianic] rectification will have to be prepared, even visibly, before the end of the present cycle; but this can only be done by one who, by uniting in himself the powers of Heaven and Earth, of East and West, will manifest outwardly, both in the domain of knowledge and in that of action, the twin sacerdotal and royal power that has been preserved across the ages in the integrity of its unique principle by the hidden keepers of the primordial tradition.

And Martin Lings, in *The Eleventh Hour*, says the following about the 'restoration' or 'brief millennium':

After 'an imminent world-wide devastation, not total, but nonetheless of cataclysmic proportions, and not final, because it is 'before the end', though there are grounds for conviction that 'the end' itself cannot be far off, there is reason to anticipate a 'redress before the close of the cycle,' based in part on the prophecy in Matt. 24 referring to the 'great tribulation such as was not since the beginning of the world,' especially in view of verse 22: 'And except those days should be shortened, there should be no flesh saved: but for the elect's sake those days shall be shortened.'

One would think that the Shiïte Muslim account of the advent, battles, final triumph and just rule of the Mahdi would be purely chiliastic, since Shiïsm, perhaps more than any other tradition except the Judaic one, conceives of the eschatological event as a revolution against tyranny (though such a revolution is also a clear subtext in the Christian *Apocalypse*). And in many ways the attribution of chiliasm to Shiïte Islam is justified. According to one account, for example, the Mahdi, or his successor, will rule for 309 years. 309, however, is also the number of years the legendary Seven Sleepers of Ephesus remained in their cave in a state of suspended animation, which would lead me to suspect that this time-period may be a veiled reference to a posthumous state. Another account gives his rule as 19 years; a Sunni account says 5, 7, or 9 years. He will die 40 days prior to the resurrection of the dead and the Day of Judgement. (A related tradition of the 'brief millennium' states that upon his second advent, Jesus will reign for 40 years after slaying Antichrist, and then die.)

It is also possible to interpret the Shiïte 'millennium', as well as the Christian one (Rev. 20:1–10), as a 'kingdom' not of this world. Jafar al-Sadiq is reported as saying, according to one source, that the Mahdi will rule for 7 years, and according to another that the rule of al-Mahdi will be as long as heaven and earth endure, and all his subjects will be in either heaven or hell—a fairly clear though veiled reference to a posthumous state. The same source quotes him to the effect that after the rule of the Mahdi will come the day of resurrection. If his rule is a posthumous one, however, this 'resurrection' must refer to the *mahapralaya*, the re-absorption of even the highest formal paradises into their Absolute Principle.

The concept of a brief millennium can perhaps also be discerned in the Old Testament book of Joel:

> The floors shall be full of wheat, and the vats shall overflow with wine and oil. And I will restore to you the years that the locust hath eaten. . . . (2:24–25) And it shall come to pass afterward that I will pour out my spirit upon all flesh; and your sons and your daughters shall prophesy, your old men shall dream dreams, your young men shall see visions: And also upon the servants and upon the handmaids in those days will I pour out my spirit. And I will show wonders in the heavens and in the earth, blood, and fire, and pillars of smoke. he sun shall be turned into darkness, and the moon into blood, before the great and terrible day of the Lord come. And it shall come to pass that whosoever shall call on the name of the Lord shall be delivered. . . . (2:28–32)

But what, if any, is the organic relationship between the idea of a brief millennial flowering immediately before the end of the cycle, suggesting the brief, terminal rally that a dying person will often exhibit, and a posthumous 'kingdom' which will have no end? The answer will be obvious to anyone who has experienced the atmosphere of joyous liberation and infinite possibility accompanying a cultural renaissance which has finally arrived after a long period of imaginative repression, or the rising portents and opening shots of a truly just social revolution, no matter how destructive the effects of these developments may ultimately be, several decades or centuries down the line. The experience is precisely that of a breakthrough of Eternity into passing time. The days of the Round Table are always short, but the Throne of Arthur, in Avalon, remains. In this world, a moment is over in an instant; in the next world, which is within this world in Essence as well as ahead of it in time, this moment has no end.

END AND BEGINNING
ARE IN GOD'S HANDS

People in the New Age movement, as well as many who are simply secularists, often believe that anyone holding the doctrine that this world must end actually wants it to end. They think of traditional eschatology as a negative self-fulfilling prophecy that prevents humanity from facing and solving global problems, and look at religious believers as spiteful maniacs who want everything to be destroyed just so they can be proved right. In some cases this may be true. But still, all that has a beginning in time also has an end. Is it a sign of mental illness to admit this? Is every person who admits, for example, that all who are born must die, necessarily depressed or suicidal?

In Chapter Ten of *Ultimate Things*, 'Why the Devil Hates a Crowd', Dennis Engleman debunks the overpopulation problem as 'bloated-earth propaganda', and maintains that 'euphemisms like "birth control" and "reproductive services" primarily mean abortion.' He repeats the tradition, common though not dogmatic, that 'only when there are enough believers to fill the places in Heaven vacated by the fallen angels, will Christ return.'

Though his book is wonderful—I would recommend it to anyone interested in the lore of the latter days—I can't entirely agree with him here. The overpopulation problem is very real. And while the same general mindset seems to be behind both birth control and abortion, in another way they are diametrically opposed: the less available and effective birth control is, the more unwanted pregnancies there will be, and the more unwanted pregnancies, the more abortions. Abortion is clearly a great evil, which Engleman rightly compares to human sacrifice. While in my opinion it is justified in some cases, such as incestuous rape, massive deformation of the fetus or virtual certainty of the mother's death—though even here I'm uneasy—it should never be undertaken lightly. Even Ken Kesey of the LSD-scattering Merry Pranksters, in one of the *Whole Earth Catalogues* around 1970, said that the major fly in the ointment of the whole Liberal/Counterculture program was abortion.

As for the legend that Christ will return when the number of believers equals the number of fallen angels, this to me represents a subtle spiritual truth which has been dragged down to the literal level. It could be used, for example, to justify Christian polygamy, since this would increase the Christian birthrate. And if Christ will only return when there are enough Christians born, then why did St Paul teach that 'It is better not to marry'?

According to Orthodox Christian and Muslim eschatology, Antichrist will co-opt the doing of good works. Does this mean that to perform good works under the regime of Antichrist is ultimately to do evil?

Antichrist, or his system, will attempt to set up the following double bind, which in many ways is already in evidence: 'Whoever does good necessarily serves me, because all good is my property; whoever would oppose me, therefore, has no choice but to do, or allow, evil.' Preventing overpopulation is a clear good. But if the macro-solution to the population problem results in massive human rights abuses, as it apparently has in China, then this good becomes a tributary to evil. Protecting the environment is a clear good. Humanity, in Genesis, is commanded by God to 'replenish' the earth, and according to Rev. 11:18, God in the latter days will reward His 'servants the prophets' but will 'destroy them which destroy the earth.' But if protecting the environment is done according to an oppressive, materialistic or scientistic paradigm which denies the theomorphic nature of man, then this good also serves an evil end. So not every way of doing good ultimately serves the Good. If a good end does not justify evil means, neither do good proximate ends or means justify an end which is ultimately evil. Death is clearly an evil, but the loss of one's immortal soul is a fate worse than death.

Any large collective effort, such as protection of the environment or the prevention of overpopulation, will necessarily generate profiteers, and attract those who are looking for political power and economic advantage. And the final parasite on all good efforts for this cycle will be the system of Antichrist. But it will always be possible to do material good in such a way that it serves spiritual good. Any effort aimed at improving material conditions, if it is based on true compassion, and on a spiritual appreciation of the human form and the natural world as signs of God's presence and symbolic manifestations of His Nature, is a form or worship. We need not, and must not, allow the system of Antichrist to co-opt all good, to the point where, in reaction against it, we become examples of cruelty or indifference which that system can use to prove its own necessity and legitimacy. All concrete good that can be done an a basis other than that of Antichrist will undercut his power and delay his advent, giving more souls time to reject error, to discern and choose the Truth. The perennial question is: When do such efforts stop being direct expressions of the good, and start becoming attempts to seize power for the abstract purpose of establishing the good, with the result that good is dethroned and power idolized? And how far can a given group or individual, in a given place and time, take power in the name of good without starting to suppress good in the name of power? Only deep spiritual discernment, based on radical submission to God's will, can answer this question.

Perhaps the greatest area of conflict and polarization between secular and the traditional eschatologies is environmentalism. Many traditional Christians see a Neo-Pagan 'Green Socialism' which worships the material cosmos in place of the Transcendent God, and denies the theomorphic nature of man, as the price of saving the environment, and they are not willing to pay it. And many environmentalists, especially those with Neo-Pagan tendencies, believe that the very idea of Transcendence, as held by the traditional religions, is at the basis of environmental destruction. They forget that it is science and technology, not religion, which are destroying the environment, and that the roots of the present regime of science and technology are in the Neo-Pagan revival of classical learning during the Renaissance, not in the transcendentalism of the Christian Middle Ages. It is precisely the belief that this world is all there is which inflames our desire to 'have it all now', and forces us to devastate the earth in the process of getting it.

It is possible, however, to work to protect the environment, in a small way, without opting for de-humanizing and anti-spiritual macro-solutions. According to Evagrius of Pontus,

As for those who are far from God. . . . God has made it possible to come near to the knowledge of him and his love for them through the medium of creatures. These he has produced, as the letters of the alphabet, so to speak, by his power and his wisdom.

Likewise the Koran teaches that

In your creation and in all the beasts scattered on the earth there are signs for people of true faith. In the alternation of night and day, and in the provision which Allah sendeth down from the heavens whereby he quickeneth the earth after its death, and in the distribution of the winds, are signs for people who are intelligent.[9]

On the basis of doctrines like these, it is possible to perform environmental service as a liturgical or contemplative act, without exalting collective material survival above the salvation of the human soul.

But if the earth is doomed, many say, then why care for the environment? This is like saying, 'why maintain your health if you're going to die anyway? Why continue to care for an elderly mother if she doesn't have long to live?' If something or someone needs care, and we have the power to give that care, then we give it. As in the path of *karma-yoga* from the *Bhavagad-Gita*, we perform the action for its own sake—that is, for God's sake—and dedicate the fruits of the action to Him.

In Rev. 19:17–18, on the day of the eschatological combat the 'fowls that fly in the midst of heaven' are invited to feast on 'the flesh of kings, and the flesh of captains, and the flesh of mighty men . . . and the flesh of all men.' And according to 2 Pet. 3:10, 'the heavens shall pass away with a great noise, and the elements shall melt with fervent heat, the earth also and the works that are therein shall be burnt up.' But Dennis Engleman repeats the doctrine that

The 'end of this world' does not produce obliteration (except of evil) but rather restoration and renewal. 'For this world shall

9. Koran 45:4–6.

pass away by transmutation, not by absolute destruction,' wrote Blessed Augustine, 'and therefore the apostle says, "For the figure of this world passeth away" (1Cor. 7:31). The figure, therefore, passes away, not the nature.[10]

According to St Irenaeus, as quoted by St Andrew of Caesarea, 'Neither the essence nor the being of the creation will perish.' As René Guénon says in *The Reign of Quantity* (pp275, 279):

> The end now under consideration is undeniably of considerably greater importance than many others, for it is the end of a whole *Manvantara,* and so of the temporal existence of what may rightly be called a humanity, but this, it must be said once more, in no way implies the end of the terrestrial world itself, because, through the 'rectification' that takes place at the final instant, this end will itself immediately become the beginning of another *Manvantara* . . . it can be said in all truth that 'the end of a world' never is and never can be anything but the end of an illusion.

It does not appear to be strictly doctrinal, then, that all life, or even all human life, must necessarily be destroyed—or necessarily preserved—at the end of this cycle.

From the material standpoint, a few species or a number of human individuals may survive, through which life could begin again. From the spiritual standpoint, all will be destroyed and burnt up, after which the Creator will renew all things. But in order to save our souls—which is the only reason we're here on earth in the first place—we must adopt the spiritual standpoint and let the material level (which is a subset of, and subordinate to, the spiritual) take care of itself according to God's design. To be willing to face the eschatological event as the end of this cycle of manifestation, to stand ready to allow oneself and all living things to die and be reborn at the touch of the Almighty, is the door to the New Heaven and the New Earth. But to plan for one's own physical survival beyond Apocalypse, or to imagine how the race could survive in material terms, through the stockpiling of computer-tended human

10. *Ultimate Things,* p258.

genetic material in secret underground caves, or what
ever other dehumanizing high-tech survivalist fantasies may
presently be hatching in the brains of those who don't know what a
human being is because they don't believe in God, is to become a
servant of the Antichrist. God will save, destroy, and re-create life as
He will; whoever places his hopes in something other than that Will
has reserved his place in the Fire.

FACING APOCALYPSE

And I saw a new heaven and a new earth: for the first heaven and the first earth were passed away; and there was no more sea.

And I John saw the holy city, new Jerusalem, coming down from God out of heaven, prepared like a bride adorned for her husband.

And I heard a great voice out of heaven saying, Behold, the tabernacle of God is with men, and they shall be his people, and God himself shall be with them and be their God.

And God shall wipe away all tears from their eyes; and there shall be no more death, neither sorrow, nor crying, neither shall there be any more pain: for the former things are passed away.

Rev. 21:1–4

IF WE SUBSCRIBE to a spirituality that would be invalidated by an end to the world, then our spirituality is not true. The same can be said, however, for a spirituality which requires the end of the world in order to validate it. The purpose of meditation upon the end of things is twofold. First, since the possibility of the end of human existence on the material plane is an inescapable part of the quality of our time, we need to have doctrinally orthodox and spiritually fruitful ways of relating to it. Secondly, the end of things is always there, no matter what period of history we live in. All things are impermanent; death comes to all. The end of things remains a reminder that we must put our hands to the plough and accomplish our salvation while we still can, since time is always short. It is also a perennial metaphor for the true death, which is the death of the ego, and the true immortality, which is the eternity of the Rock of Ages, impervious to the waves of time, the cycles of creation, and dissolution which break against it.

According to the Traditionalists, the latter days are not without their own particular blessings and spiritual opportunities, which could exist at no other point in the cycle. The first is the comparative ease of spiritual detachment, to those who are at all inclined in that direction. In Martin Lings' words, 'Detachment is an essential feature of the sage, and this virtue, which in better times could only be acquired through great spiritual efforts, can be made more spontaneous by the sight of one's world in chaotic ruins.'

The second blessing is that of encyclopedic knowledge. 'If human societies degenerate on the one hand with the passage of time,' says Schuon, 'they accumulate on the other hand experiences in virtue of old age, however intermingled with errors these may be.' Knowledge of the great spiritual traditions of the world, such as made possible the writing of this book, was much more difficult to access even a few decades ago.

The third blessing, in this extreme old age of the macrocosm, is the enhanced possibility of spiritual serenity and insight. In *The Eleventh Hour*, Martin Lings writes:

There is . . . a feature of normal old age, the most positive of all . . . in virtue of which our times are unique. It is sometimes said of spiritual men and women at the end of their lives that they have 'one foot already in Paradise.' This is not meant to deny that death is a sudden break, a rupture of continuity. It cannot but be so, for it has to transform mortal old age into immortal youth. None the less, hagiography teaches that the last days of sanctified souls can be remarkably luminous and transparent. Nor is it unusual that the imminence of death should bring with it special graces, such as visions, in foretaste of what is to come. The mellowing of spirituality, which is the highest aspect of old age itself, is thus crowned with an illumination which belongs more to youth than to age . . . in the macrocosm, the nearness of the new Golden Age cannot fail to make itself mysteriously felt before the end of the old cycle. . . . (p 66)

THE SYSTEM OF ANTICHRIST

According to Rev. 20:7–8,

> When the thousand years are expired [the millennium during which the devil is bound, identified by Orthodox theologians as the church age], Satan shall be loosed out of his prison, and shall go out to deceive the nations which are in the four quarters of the earth, Gog and Magog, to gather them together to battle: the number of whom is as the sand of the sea.'

According to *The Apocalypse of St John: An Orthodox Commentary* by Archbishop Averky of Jordanville, the meaning of *Gog* in Hebrew is 'a gathering' or 'one who gathers', and of *Magog* 'an exaltation' or 'one who exalts'. 'Exaltation' suggests to me the idea of transcendence as *opposed* to unity, 'gathering' the idea of unity as *opposed* to transcendence. The implication, here, is that one of the deepest deceptions of Antichrist in the last days of the cycle will be to set these two integral aspects of the Absolute in opposition to each other in the collective mind, and on a global scale, in 'the four quarters of the earth'. As for the economic and political expression of this barren satanic polarity, the false cohesion of left-wing tyranny, as well as today's global capitalism, would fall under Gog, while both the false hierarchicalism of right-wing tyranny and the violent absolutism of the various 'tribal' separatist movements opposed to globalism, both ethnic and religious, would come under Magog. In terms of religion, those liberal, historicist, evolutionist, quasi-materialist and crypto-Pagan theologies which emphasize God's immanence as opposed to His transcendence are part of Gog, while those reactionary theologies which exalt transcendence over immanence, look on the material world as a vale of tears, denigrate the human body, and view the destruction of nature with indifference if not secret approval, since the best we can hope for is to get it all over with, are part of Magog. The conflict between the two is precisely the satanic counterfeit of the true eschatological conflict described in Rev. 19:11–20, between the King of Kings and Lord of Lords, and the Beast with his false prophet. Those who can be lured to fight in a counterfeit war between elements which ought to be reconciled, because they are essentially parts of the same reality as seen in a distorting mirror, will miss their call to fight in the true war between forces which neither should nor can be reconciled: those of the Truth and those of the Lie. (Note: Globalism, insofar as it sets the stage for the emergence of Guénon's 'inverted hierarchy', also contains the seed of Magog, while tribalism, as the common inheritance of all who are excluded from the global elite, holds the seed of Gog; in the latter days, no party or class or sector can long retain its ideological stability; the 'rate of contradiction' approaches the speed of light.)

In a world profoundly polarized between the Gog of syncretist globalism and the Magog of exclusivist 'tribalism'—a word which is beginning to denote what used to be called 'nationalism' or 'patriotism' or 'loyalty to one's religion'—the Transcendent Unity of Religions clearly represents a middle path, or third force, at least in the religious field. It is equally opposed to the universalism of the global elites and the violent self-assertion of the fundamentalist 'tribes' oppressed and marginalized by these elites. Perhaps this is one reason why groups and individuals who hold to this doctrine have been subjected to the immense degree of psychic pressure which observers on the outskirts of the Traditionalist School, such as myself, cannot fail to note. It is reasonable to conjecture that Antichrist would like nothing better than to subvert and discredit the Traditionalists, since the Transcendent Unity of Religions is one of the few worldviews that could possibly stand in the way of the barren and terminal conflict between globalism and tribalism which is the keynote of his 'system' in the social arena.

If all possible alternatives to the struggle between globalism and tribalism disappear from the collective mind, then Antichrist has won. He can use economic and political globalism and the universalism of a 'world fusion spirituality' to subvert and oppress all integral religions and religious cultures, forcing them to narrow their focus and violate the fullness of their own traditions in reaction against it. He can drive them to bigoted and terroristic excesses which will make them seem barbaric and outdated in the eyes of those wavering between a global and a tribal identification, and set them at each other's throats at the same time. Unite to oppress; divide and conquer.

In this light, we can see that the exclusivism of conservative and/ or traditional Christianity is both its greatest strength and its greatest weakness; the same could be said, with certain reservations, of Judaism and Islam. The exclusivism of these Abrahamic religions allows them to consciously fortify themselves against the System of Antichrist—Christianity by its 'catacomb spirit', its ability, ultimately derived from monasticism, to build spiritual fortresses against the world, and Islam by the fact that *dar al-Islam* remains the largest bloc of humanity which, in part, is still socially and politically organized around a Divine Revelation, although to greatly varying degrees, as were Medieval Europe and the Byzantine Empire. On the other hand, their very exclusivism has prevented these religions, in all but a few instances, from making common cause against globalist universalism and secularism. They remain vulnerable to the 'divide and conquer' tactics of the system of Antichrist, a phase which could well be the prelude, if traditional eschatological speculations such as those found in Dennis E. Engleman's *Ultimate Things* are to be believed, to a later 'unite to oppress' phase—a capitulation by the exhausted exclusivists, longing for the end of endless conflict, to the satanic universalism of Antichrist himself.

According to *Ultimate Things*, Antichrist will reveal himself in Jerusalem and proclaim himself King of the Jews; the Jewish nation, as well as many Christians, will accept him. From the Islamic perspective, however, any world ruler who begins as a King of the Jews and is later submitted to by the Christians would be immediately and universally recognized as Antichrist himself. It is inconceivable, unless traditional and even fundamentalist Islam were to virtually disappear, that such a figure could tempt Muslims to accept him as the Mahdi or the eschatological Jesus. So if the predictions Engleman recounts are in any way accurate, he is in fact presenting, as the most likely eschatological scenario, a mass apostasy of Jews and Christians which would leave only the Muslims aware of who Antichrist really is, and ready to do battle with him. How then could Antichrist emerge as a true global monarch, albeit a satanic one?

Perhaps the militant opposition of an Islam discredited in the eyes of the rest of the world to an almost universally admired 'savior' is the very thing which will ultimately consolidate his power. I hasten to say that this is in no way a prediction; God forbid. I am simply allowing myself to imagine various scenarios based on the quality of ultimate irony and self-contradiction which is the keynote of all historical forces in these latter days. And one of the twists of this irony is the fact that many semi-secularized Muslims—Dodi al-Fayed, for example—seem much more in tune with the mores of postmodern globalist culture than any Christian I could name.

If the greatest strength and greatest weakness of traditional Christianity is in its exclusivism, the comparable strength and weakness of Buddhism, especially in the West), is in its ability to 'fit in'. (The same goes for heterodox Westernized Hinduism and various influences, such as Feng Shui, Taoist meditation, and Sino-Japanese martial arts, originating in the Far East.) At its best, this represents a radical detachment from the norms of 'the world', allowing it to avoid all forms of dogmatic literalism and fundamentalism, and the marginalization such a stance often entails. At its worst, it indicates a capitulation to the collective egotism of this very 'world'. In the United States at least, Buddhism is an acceptable part of the general Neo- Pagan cultural drift, which, while it may not identify with globalism, nonetheless often ends by serving it. (The same is true of certain strands of American Sufism, especially those which attempt to separate the Sufi tradition from Islam.) As a religion which recognizes a fall (into ignorance) and posits a goal of salvation (via enlightenment), it 'naturally' has a much greater affinity with the Abrahamic religions than with a Paganism which accepts the ontological status quo and seeks only to profit from it. But that's not how things have worked out sociologically. American Buddhism, as a non-theistic religion (though certainly not an atheism, since it possesses a doctrine of the Absolute), has been attractive to many people—especially, as it turns out, many American Jews—who are in flight from their own narrow-minded and superstitious ideas of God. An acquaintance of mine, a traditional Catholic who studied for years under the Hopi elders, tells the story of a 'Buddhist Halloween party' where a well-known American Buddhist teacher, dressed as a 'Sufi', made the statement that Buddhism is better than the Abrahamic religions because, just like the Native Americans, the Buddhists don't believe in God—a statement which my friend knew, from long personal experience with Native American spirituality, to be totally false. It was nonetheless an idea which would 'play well' to the general liberal, New Age and Neo-Pagan culture from which this teacher draws his students, the kind of people whose appreciation for the American Indians is even more destructive to Native American spirituality than their attraction to Buddhism is to Buddhism.

The false ecumenism of Neo-Pagan, New Age culture is the seed-bed for that 'world fusion spirituality' in which fragments of every spiritual tradition are promiscuously thrown together, to their mutual corruption. True ecumenism on the other hand—the outer expression of the 'esoteric ecumenism' of the Transcendent Unity of Religions, which understands the very uniqueness and particularity of the authentic religious traditions as the transcendent basis for their unity—is not a syncretistic amalgam or a diplomatic glossing-over of doctrinal differences, but a united front against a common enemy: that unholy alliance of scientism, magical materialism, idolatry of the psyche and postmodern nihilism which is headed, with all deliberate speed, toward the system of Antichrist.

Leo Schaya, writing primarily from the standpoint of Jewish esoterism, sees the eschatological mission of Elias as a re-establishment of the 'unanimous tradition' in preparation for the advent of the Messiah. Before the event known in *Genesis* as the 'confusion of tongues' which followed the fall of the Tower of Babel, humanity spoke a single religious language. After that time, however, God's Self-revelation to Man took the form of discrete religious traditions, each one self-enclosed and self-sufficient. The Tree of Life, which had been a single trunk, now divided into several branches. According to Schaya, however, the primordial unanimity is destined to be re-established before the end of the cycle:

> According to Jewish tradition, the entire Torah of Moses amounts to no more than a single line of the *Sepher ha-Yasher* [the 'Book of Justice' which Elias must bring with him], which means that this Book, by virtue of not being 'scriptural' but

'operative' in nature, will be the veritable final accomplishment of Scripture, the 'realization' which by definition goes immeasurably beyond the 'letter'. At the same time, Judaism tacitly places the remaining 'lines' of this 'Book' at the disposal of all the Divine revelations, whatever they may be, each one formulating or announcing in its fashion the same Eternal Truth and the same Destiny of man and the world. The 'Book' of Elias is the integral Wisdom of the unanimous Tradition and the eschatological Manifestation of the one and only Principle. For the Jews, Elias represents the transition from traditional exclusiveness to the universality which they too possess, since they affirm that the Tishbite will raise his voice so loud to announce the spiritual peace that it will be heard from one end of the earth to the other; and the Doctors of the Law teach that 'the righteous of all nations have a portion in the life to come' or, again, that 'all men who are not idolaters can be considered Israelites.'

Elias must re-establish all things in the name of, and for the sake of, that spiritual 'peace' which the Messiah will bring once and for all: it will be crystallized forever in the New Jerusalem 'founded by—or for—peace', according to the etymology of *Yerushalem* or *Yerushalaim*. Elias came down, and has come down for centuries, to the world below to prepare, with the concurrence of those he inspires, this final state of humanity. He reveals, little by little and more intensively and generally toward the end, the spiritual and universal essence, the transcendent unity of all authentic religions. It is as if the radiant city were being patiently built by putting one luminous stone after another into place. The motivating power of this task can be called the 'Eliatic flow', at least in the orbit of the Judeo-Christian tradition, whereas other traditions will each use their own terms to describe this same universal flow. According to the terminology of Jewish esoterism, this flow belongs to the 'river of highest Eden', the 'river of Yobel' or 'great Jubilee' which is final Deliverance. Apocalypse calls it 'the river of the water of life, clear as crystal' Rev. 22:1); it will be crystallized in the 'precious stones', the unquenchable lights of the New Jerusalem.[1]

The doctrine of 'the Book of Elias' is strictly paralleled by the Shiïte Muslim doctrine that when al-Mahdi emerges from his occultation he will bring a new Book. That this Book represents the Primordial Tradition itself, which transcends the revealed traditions without negating them, is indicated by the tradition that the Mahdi will 'rule the people of the Torah according to the Torah, and the people of the Gospel according to the Gospel, and the people of the Koran according to the Koran.' (Nasir al-Din Tusi, *Ghayba*). That the Mahdi will restore the scriptures of Adam and Seth, and tear down the Kaaba so as to rebuild it as it was in Adam's time, also refers to the Primordial Tradition. The same order of truth is perhaps symbolized in Rev. 7:4–8 by the '144,000 sealed' who are drawn (12,000 at a time, like the 12,000 followers of Ali who will rise from the dead to follow the Mahdi) from each of the twelve tribes of Israel, and who in this context cannot be strictly identified with the Jews, but must represent twelve separate facets of the human form, and also by the fact that the Heavenly Jerusalem will contain no temple, 'for the Lord God Almighty and the Lamb are the temple of it' (Rev. 21:22–23). In the words of Jesus, 'other sheep have I.'

The prophecy that the primordial unity of religious truth will be re-established before the end can also be found in the Zoroastrian tradition. According to the *Vendidad* (2),*Yima*, the first man, the Zoroastrian Adam, was the human being to whom Ahura Mazda first preached the Ahuric or Zoroastrian religion; likewise Jews and Muslims, on the same plane of understanding, see Adam not only as the first man but also the first prophet. After expanding, cultivating and ruling the world of manifestation for (as I read it) 1,800 years, Yima was summoned by Ahura Mazda, who predicted that bad winters would come to the material world, one of which would be especially destructive. (This is substantially the same doctrine as the eschatological *Fimbulwinter* of Norse mythology; the name *Yima* is

also related to the Norse *Ymir*, the original giant who was slaugh-
tered to create the material world, whose bones became the mountains, whose blood the rivers, etc.). Ahura Mazda then commanded
Yima to build a *var* ('enclosure') with a square floor-plan, stock it
with golden hay, and gather into it the seed of the best plants, the
best animals, the best human beings, 1800 persons in all, as well as
the sun, moon and stars, which, in the var, can be seen setting and
rising only once a year. However, to the inhabitants of the var, each
day will be as a year. (1800 x 80 = 144,000, the number of the elect in
the New Jerusalem.) There is to be a river watering the var, which
will also contain meadows, houses—the whole manifest world in
microcosm.

The Var of Yima, then, is the Zoroastrian equivalent of Noah's
ark, though the world-destroying catastrophe is seen as a freeze
rather than a flood. It is also similar in some ways to the New Jerusalem, which is likewise four-square and watered by a river. Yima's
Var, however, seems to be underground; it is an enclosure, a cave,
and also an ancient subterranean kingdom, like the Celtic realm of
'faerie', whose denizens reside in 'fairy hills'—the barrow tombs
which dot the Western European landscape; as such, it is analogous
to the *kiva* of the Ant People of Hopi myth. (The birthplace of
Christ in a stable or cave surrounded by animals, his crib a manger
filled with hay, and his visitation by three 'wise men' who are usually considered to have been Zoroastrian Magi, would tend to identify him with Yima, at least in the eyes of Zoroastrians, but also
perhaps to those Jews, such as the Essenes, who may have main-
tained ongoing Zoroastrian connections.)

According to the story, Yima's Var was designed to help humanity
and nature survive a series of hard winters; yet it is also said that
the Var of Yima will only be opened at Frashegird, the end of time.
So it becomes clear that the 'hard winters' actually represent the
freezing and contraction of the cosmic environment, including
human perception, which must worsen as the cycle unfolds. As
Blake identified Noah's flood as an overwhelming of the Atlantean
Golden Age by 'the Sea of Space and Time', so the 'bad winters' of
Zoroastrian myth represent in some ways the increasing materialism
of human society, and the consequent relegation of the vision of

Eternity to a mythological underground kingdom. 'Underground' equals 'repressed'; what was once an immediate sensual vision of the natural world *sub specie aeternitatis* is now hidden away, for safe-keeping, in 'the cave of the Heart'.

In 1927, Guénon published a book entitled *Le Roi du Monde*, 'The King of the World'. It dealt with the myth of the sacred Center in various religions (Mecca, Jerusalem, Olympus, etc.) and posited the existence of a Primordial Center, an original Hyperborean Paradise, from which all others derive, an assertion which has led some to criticize him for indulging, like Gurdjieff and Idries Shah, in occult-ist geographical romanticism of the 'Shangri-La' variety—Shangri-La itself, of course, being a late literary rendition of the same myth of Hyperborea, the land of eternal spring which lies in the extreme North, 'behind the North Wind'. This original Center is the source of the Primordial Tradition, whose representative, in terms of the Abrahamic religions, is Melchizedek. In the book of *Genesis*, Melchizedek, King of Salem and Priest of the most high God, blesses Abraham, in what Guénon identifies as a ceremony of initia-tion. Melchizedek is also mentioned in Ps. 110:4: 'The Lord swore and will not repent: thou art a priest forever after the order of Melchizedek.' Jesus comments upon this psalm in *Mark* and *Luke*, as does Peter in his Pentecost sermon as recounted in *Acts*. Guénon compares Melchizedek with the Hindu Manu, and other original priests and lawgivers.

It is fairly clear that the Zoroastrian Yima is another version of this 'King of the World'. The Sufis too have a concept of 'The Pole of the Age'—obviously a Hyperborean symbol—which is similar in many ways to the Shiïte doctrine of the Mahdi, the occulted Twelfth Imam; Shiïte esoterism in fact identifies the Mahdi with Melchizedek. The lineage of this unknown Pole, or *Qutub*, would therefore appear to be the Sufi version of the primordial priesthood of Melchizedek, who, since he had no father or mother, is in a certain sense immortal: unborn, thus never to die. This places him in the same category as the 'immortal prophets' Enoch, Elias and the Sufi Khidr, 'the Green One', identified by Muslims with both Elias and St George. As Melchizedek was Abraham's master in the Old Testament, so Khidr is the name given by Sufis to the master encountered by Moses in the Koran. The King of the World also has obvious affinities with figures such as Arthur, and all the other 'once and future kings' of world mythology. Arthur's knight Owain, in the romance of 'Owain and the Countess of the Fountain' becomes master of the Fountain of Life; the same is true of many of the sacred kings mentioned in Frazer's *The Golden Bough*, and of Khidr as well, who guards the Fountain of Life which is placed 'between the two seas', on the *barzakh* (isthmus) between this world and the next—in one sense the subtle or *faerie* realm, in another sense the Heart, situated between the bitter waters material multiplicity and the sweet waters of spiritual Unity. The Heavenly Jerusalem also encloses the Fountain of Life.

The Var of Yima is identified as the Hyperborean Paradise by the fact that it contains sun, moon and stars, which once a year (or once a day) can be seen setting and rising. Facing south in the Northern Hemisphere (i.e., looking out from the North), one is in a position to view the points where the sun and moon rise and set; facing north, one can view the stars rising and setting simultaneously. The celestial aspect of the Var of Yima is thus revealed in the constellations of the Great and Little Bear, the Revolving Castle or *caer sidi* of the Byrthonic Celts where departed kings consort with the White Goddess, in endless motion about the Pole Star (the *Qutub*), that 'still point of the turning world' which is the visible pivot of Eternity in the created order, the door which leads beyond the cycles of birth and death. (Guénon, in *Science of Sacred Symbols*, claims that *var* and *bear* are the same word.) The fact that the Var contains the seeds of all living things, including the circling heavens, indicates that it is not only a Temple but also an Aeon: an entire cycle of manifestation witnessed simultaneously as a single form. The Tree of Life in the New Jerusalem, which bears twelve kinds of fruit, one each month—an obvious reference to the zodiac—has the same meaning: a complete cycle of time conceived in a single moment.

The Lakota Sioux call south 'the direction we always face', and in so doing identify themselves as Hyperboreans, whose seat is in the North, beyond the cycles of time, from which point they look South into this material world. They further identify the north-south axis as 'the good red road' and the east-west line of the Sun's track as 'the black (or blue) road of difficulty.' Shamanism in general can be described as a Hyperborean spirituality. Not only is its home in the far North (Siberia), but the 'axial' structure of Siberian shamanism, according to which the shaman ascends and/or descends the World Tree, up through many paradises or down through many underworlds, like the angels ascending and descending the ladder in Jacob's dream, reveals it as a Polar manifestation. (Sometimes the shaman will use an actual ladder during his trance.) A poem from the Altaic tradition, adapted from Mircea Eliade's *Shamanism: Archaic Techniques of Ecstasy*, speaks of a shamanic journey to a 'Prince Ulgan' who lives in the sky, and who is described as the one 'for whom the stars & sky/are turning a thousand times/turning a thousand times over'—a Siberian version of the transcendent God as 'the King of the World' in his celestial 'var'. In the same poem the shaman is shown climbing the sky in the shape of a goose. Migrating geese, who in Celtic mythology are identified with the souls of the dead (and, undoubtedly, the unborn), follow the north-south Hyperborean path, the Good Red Road, which is a projection onto the horizontal plane of the *axis mundi*, the vertical path uniting Heaven and Earth. This path is identified with, among other things, the human spinal column: in Yoga terminology, the *sushumna nadi* with its seven *chakras*. *Paramhamsa* or 'exalted gander' is also an epithet of Hindu yogis.

This North-South orientation places Hyperborean spirituality on a higher ontological plane than those religions whose sacred point of 'orientation' is the East. Facing East we witness all forms and events as they enter the cycle of manifestation from the Unseen; facing West, we watch as they leave it. But if we face North, we are oriented to that Eternal Center which is beyond manifestation entirely; it is as if, instead of turning within the cycles of birth and death, those cycles were to turn within us. Hyperborean religion is thus Edenic and Primordial. When Adam and Eve were cast out of Paradise, they traveled to 'the East of Eden'; this, in my opinion, represents a fall from an aeonian and Hyperborean North-facing spirituality to a cyclical and Solar East-facing one—in Lakota terms, a departure from the Good Red Road to walk the Black Road of Difficulty (cf. Gen. 3:19: 'In the sweat of thy face thou shall eat bread').

And the fact that, in so many ancient traditions, demonic forces are pictured as coming out of the North indicates both the rigor of Transcendence, and the fact that the way back to Hyperborea, in this cycle, is closed; the gates of Eden are blocked by the Cherubim and the flaming sword which turns every way (Gen. 3:24). The seat of the Tribe of Dan, for example, from whom the Antichrist is supposed to emerge, is in the extreme north of Israel. In other words, we can't ignore time; we must conform our spirituality to the needs of the particular point in the cycle where we find ourselves, or risk invoking demonic energies. And this means, among other things, that shamanism is not what it used to be. To practice it this late in the cycle, especially if one is not born into one of the primal religions, is to encounter spiritual dangers which did not exist when the cycle was young. Undoubtedly some of the primal traditions are still host to powerful, balanced shamans dedicated to spiritual enlightenment and human service—and God knows best.

According to Guénon, Melchizedek represents the Primordial Tradition for the Abrahamic religions; but it is probably simpler and more enlightening to say that the King of the World is *Adam*, in line with the Muslim doctrine that man is not only God's *abd* or slave, but also His *khalifa* or vice-regent. The metaphysical principle, here, is that since every fall is from a relatively more real and more eternal plane of being to a relatively less real and more temporal one, there is always a sense in which the fall in question never took place; a fall into illusion is always, in *one* sense, illusory. (Herman Hesse's novel *Journey to the East* is all about this.) As the Buddhists say, 'all beings are enlightened from the beginning.' So the Adam who never fell, the archetype of Man in the subtle material plane, who is Yima, the Hindu Manu, and Melchizedek, is, in a way, still ruling us. If he were not still there on the subtle plane we would not still be here on the material plane, since he is part of our 'stem', our living and ongoing connection with our Creator via the Unseen World. The question is, can we turn to him as a 'Pole' in any real and spiritually effective sense? Much water has flowed under the bridge since the Golden Age, and it keeps flowing faster and faster. Primordial spiritualities can still look to that one who is called by the Mandaeans of Iraq 'the Secret Adam', but historical man is not primordial now, except in essence. The cycle has moved on; we have entered the world of fall and redemption, and so must turn to saviors instead, prophets like Abraham, Moses and Muhammad, avatars like Rama, or Krishna, or Jesus. Certainly religions still exist which look back to the Primordial Ancestor rather than to the Savior, already come or yet-to-come, as their spiritual focus; this is true of many African religions and of totemism in general, as it was of the ancient Chinese worship of the Yellow Emperor. But virtually all these religions show signs of serious degeneration. And the lateness of the hour is further reflected, in a way I take to be normative, by the fact that the cult of Brahma the Creator has essentially died out in Hinduism; Hindu devotees now look either to Vishnu the Preserver or Shiva the Destroyer. Furthermore, history has proceeded so far toward the end of the aeon that the expected advent of Kalki, or Maitreya, or al-Mahdi, or the eschatological Christ begins to exert its magnetic attraction, and become our new spiritual Center. Cyclically speaking, this leaves the primordial Adam far behind.

And yet eternity is never 'behind'. The truth that Adam, in a specific sense, never really fell, will always be there in the background of this fallen world. It is in some ways closer in Islam than in Christianity, at least Western Christianity, since Muslims do not recognize a total fall of man, a corruption of the human substance itself, but only *ghaflah*, 'heedlessness', the Platonic *amnesia*—though the consequences of this heedlessness are as dire as those of any original sin. In Islam, a human being can still stand as Adam before God, in his original unfallen nature, his *fitrah*. But as Blake shows through his figure of Albion the Ancient Man, the King of the World is, in a very real sense, fallen or deposed. Within the Christian universe, he needs Christ to redeem him; this is what is meant by 'the harrowing of hell' which follows the crucifixion and precedes the resurrection. (Yima, too, is fallen in one way, unfallen and eternal in another.) As in Blake's *Jerusalem*, Jesus must awaken Albion/Adam from his death-like sleep upon the Rock of Ages, where he lies submerged, like the lost Atlantis, beneath the Sea of Space and Time.

Guénon in *The Reign of Quantity* says that Antichrist will be a kind of inverted *Chakravartin*, a false World King. So the question inevitably arises: What does this false King have to do with the true King of the World supposedly still reigning in Shambhala/Belovodia/Avalon? Are they at war in that other world? If the King of the World is in one sense unfallen and still reigning, and in another sense deposed, and if the Antichrist is destined to appear as a false World King, then exactly what is the eschatological role of *le Roi du Monde*?

In C.S. Lewis' *That Hideous Strength* a war is fought between the powers of Light and Darkness to see if the ancient Pagan magic represented by Merlin—who himself had no human father, and who never died (like Elias, Enoch, Khidr, and the Twelfth Imam) but was 'occulted'—will fall under the power of the forces of Truth, or those of Antichrist. If we take Merlin as representing the Primordial Tradition, at least to Lewis (who furthermore relates Merlin to the priesthood of Melchizedek), we can support him in his intuition that the remnants of certain archaic spiritualities can and will support the forces of Light in the eschatological combat: According to the relevant Zoroastrian doctrine, during Frashegird the Var of Yima will be opened; its inhabitants will emerge and join the cosmic struggle until the final triumph of the good. So primordiality joins forces with eschatology, just as one's original nature as created by God joins forces with redemption and divine Grace; Yima supports Saoshyant; the first 'savior' fights by the side of the last. In the same way, Shiïte eschatology envisions a return of the most righteous as well as the most unrighteous of the dead before the general resurrection, giving the righteous an opportunity to triumph at last over their oppressors. The most common epithet of the Shiïte Mahdi, *al-Qaim*, 'he who rises', denotes both the resurrection of the dead and to a 'rising up' against tyranny. When John the Baptist, dressed in animal skins and eating gathered rather than cultivated food, announced the advent of Jesus Christ, I believe he was consciously enacting the part of the Primordial Adam (possibly in his Essene/Mandean rendition) as herald and ally of the Savior.

Since the eschatological event is a breakthrough of Eternity into time, it has to include all the manifestations of Divine Truth comprised within the cycle which is coming to a close; it must be a summing up as well as a death and rebirth. The emphasis of the

Traditionalist writers on the Primordial Tradition and the Transcendent Unity of Religions is therefore a necessary and providential expression of spiritual truth for these latter days.

TO FIGHT OR NOT TO FIGHT

The looming One World Government shows many signs of being the predicted regime of Antichrist. But as I have already pointed out, it's not quite that simple, since the 'tribal' forces reacting against globalism are ultimately part of the same system. According to one of many possible scenarios, the satanic forces operating at the end of the Aeon would be quite capable of establishing a One World Government only to set the stage for the emergence of Antichrist as the great leader of a world revolution *against* this government, which, if it triumphed, would be the *real* One World Government. Or the martyrdom of Antichrist at the hands of such a government might be a deliberate or even staged self-sacrifice, counterfeiting the death of Christ and leading to a counterfeit resurrection. I am not saying that this will happen; I am not prognosticating. I only wish to point out that Antichrist, as a counterfeit manifestation of the Divine universality, will have the capacity to use all sides in any conflict, including a global one, to build his power—except the ultimate Messianic Conflict, called Armageddon in the *Apocalypse*, which is initiated and concluded by God Himself.

The 'discernment of spirits' in apocalyptic times can perhaps be reduced to the ability to answer, in many different circumstances, a single question: *what is the real war?* If the Antichrist can tempt us to fight prematurely, or on too restricted a field—or, conversely, if he can influence us to delay too long before choosing sides—then he has won. Here, however, is the danger of the approach I have taken, that of multiplying the criteria by which the coming Avatara can be distinguished from Antichrist. The danger is that we may become stuck in a kind of paranoid infinite regression, as in the world of espionage where every double agent is really a triple agent and things are never what they seem. Because, in another sense, things are always what they seem—to the pure in heart. If you know your own ego, you know the Antichrist; if you know the God within you, you know God. The criteria by which we can recognize the Antichrist are the same as those by which we can recognize sin: If we understand what Divine Wisdom is, we will recognize what is contrary to that Wisdom; if we know what Divine Love is, we will be sensitive to what violates that Love. The signs of the end in the various traditional eschatologies cannot be applied directly to history, without first being applied to the state of one's soul. Only after 'the discernment of spirits' is established within our own intellect, will, and affections can we turn and see the forces operating in these latter days of world history in the light of objective truth. If we know how the ego operates, especially when it attempts to appropriate our struggle against temptation in order to claim holiness for itself, or break its way into the mysteries of God in order to claim wisdom, then we will not be fooled by the analogous moves of the Antichrist on the field of history.

Antichrist's ability to fight simultaneously on all sides in a war in order to spread delusion, paranoia and self-perpetuating conflict, which is a satanic parody of God's hidden presence behind every human mask, is perhaps nowhere better illustrated than in contemporary Israel. Every act of oppression and/or legitimate self-defense by the Israeli government, every act of terrorism and/or legitimate self-protection by the Palestinian 'extremists', every act of self-contradictory 'moderation' by the PLO, and every act of intervention and/or neglect by Iran, Russia, Egypt, Syria, Lebanon, Jordan, the United States, Western Europe, or the U.N., produces—after a certain point—the identical effect: the hardening of lines, the escalation of conflict. This is not to say that some lines of action are not better than others, only that the situation has a life of its own, and possesses the power to impose its tax upon all conceivable ways of relating to it.

It is quite astounding to realize that, according to one view of the situation, the same socio-political 'slots' exist in Palestine today as in the time of Jesus, two thousand years ago, though they are occupied by profoundly different forces. The Israeli Government stands where the Scribes and Pharisees then stood. The militant Palestinians occupy the niche of the Zealots. The United States and/or the

U.N. can stand-in for the Roman Empire. And the unique position of Jesus, at the crux or *cross* where all contemporary social forces converged, is now occupied by Yasser Arafat, crucified as he is on the horns of every contradiction... but clearly Arafat is no Jesus; he in no way transcends the conditions he occupies; he is merely the puppet of them.

Jesus of Nazareth was deeply aware of contemporary political forces. On the human level, he had to be. This did not mean, of course, that he was some kind of political revolutionary; he may in fact have needed a certain political savvy simply to avoid being forced to take sides—for or against the party of the Temple in its accommodation with Rome, for or against the Zealots—in a world where everyone apparently had to take sides, where everything was moving inexorably toward the Jewish Revolt of AD 66 For example, when his opponents challenged him to answer, in public, whether or not it was lawful to pay the Roman tax, they thought they had him. If he had said 'yes', he would lose his following in the Zealot sector, who, because they interpreted the tax an act of emperor-worship, which had been officially established in some Roman provinces, considered it a blasphemy against Yahweh, especially since the Roman denarius in which the tax was to be paid bore an image of the emperor, seen by the Zealots as an idol, a 'graven image'. He would also have lost his moral authority to criticize the Scribes and Pharisees, who had made an accommodation with the Roman colonial government. He would have been drawn into the party of the temple authorities, at least in the eyes of the people, which would have alienated him from both the Zealots and the Essenes. On the other hand, if he said 'no', he would have been simply identified with the Zealots, and would have lost touch with his wider public. He would also have been liable to premature arrest on a provable charge of sedition; consequently his death would have meant no more than the death of, say, someone like Barabbas. Like thousands of other, he would have died as a 'one-dimensional' rebel against Rome, and been forgotten.

His way of passing through the 'symplegades' of this socio-political contradiction represented a masterpiece of 'sublimation', and may give us a clue as to how to avoid being drawn into false or narrowly-defined conflicts, and travel instead the path which leads to the true war. First, he asked someone in the crowd to hand him the coin of tribute, thus demonstrating, first, that he had no money himself, that he was of the 'poor' to whom he came to preach the 'good news'—in Arabic, *fuqara*, the plural of *fakir* which is synonymous with 'Sufi'—and secondly that the 'idolatrous' coin in question was in free circulation. Secondly, when he asked 'whose image is this?' and was answered 'Caesar's,' he was distancing himself from the Zealots by clearly demonstrating that the coin could not be an idol for the simple reason that Caesar was not God, which is why one could render to Caesar what was Caesar's without committing blasphemy. At the same time he was saying, in effect, that to send the image of the little false god back to him was in no way to worship him, but could even be seen as an act of condescension on the part of the Jews, who knew and worshipped the Living God; their self-respect, their privileged position as the chosen people could in no way be violated by humoring the petty narcissism of these little self-appointed Caesars. So without a marvelous degree of political and psychological savvy, Jesus would have inevitably been drawn into political conflict, and his mission would have failed. (This, of course, is the situation seen from the standpoint of Jesus' humanity; from the point-of-view of His Divinity, His mission was ordained by God; it could not fail.) And this object-lesson on how to avoid being drawn too far into premature and narrowly-defined political conflicts which compromise one's spiritual perception and one's readiness to heed God's true call also has its esoteric side, as a 'parable-in- action' of how to pass beyond the pairs-of-opposites and realize the Absolute. The Eastern Orthodox Christians interpret 'what is Caesar's' as the coin's weight in gold, and 'what is God's' as the shape of a human being stamped upon it, made in the image and likeness of God. The matter of our lives will always belong to this world; our wealth will pass to others, as our bodies to the earth. But our form belongs to God in eternity, unto ages of ages. This is why, in the resurrection, it is capable of being newly 'incarnated' in a glorious and incorruptible substance. The lesson is: that it is not the *matter* of our lives we must protect from the Antichrist—as certain survivalists clearly believe—but our *form*. In the latter days, as always, the real struggle is not to retain our possessions, or even our lives, but to avoid losing our souls. Ultimately, this is all that is required of us.

In a world defined by false conflicts of every kind, what is the true war? The Muslim answer is: 'The Greater Jihad, the war against everything in oneself that is opposed to God.' But the Greater and the Lesser Holy Wars—the Lesser Jihad in this case being the struggle in the outer world against all that would attack or subvert religion—are not unrelated. All we can hope for in the end times— and it is really the greatest hope humanity can ever be blessed with—is that we ourselves will remain faithful to the Truth. But sometimes, in order not to be driven away from that Truth by fear, or lured away by satanic seduction, it must be actively defended in the outer world, either by word or by deed. If we are not willing to risk our reputations, our livelihoods or our lives when circumstances demand it, how can we be sure that our inner faithfulness to God is anything more than lip service, or spiritual pride? On the other hand, if we had truly defeated the Beast within, the 'commanding self', the world's terror and seduction would have no power over us. So the Lesser Jihad, no matter how necessary in certain circumstances, is always in one sense a 'projection' of the Greater Jihad on the world stage; it is the war against the commanding self fought in allegory, and by proxy.

Perhaps the best answer to the question 'to fight or not to fight?' is: Learn to deal only with the single enemy, inner or outer, who is directly in your path. If you try to fight somebody else's battle, God will not support you. And if you depart from your own true path because you are hungry for conflict, or just impatient to get it all over with, then you have already been defeated. This is why it is so important to know your path as it really is, so you can tell the difference between God-given talents which must not be buried, and self-imposed agendas which need to be sacrificed.

The least that can be said in concrete terms is that a denunciation of the regime of Antichrist, such as that by the 'two witnesses' in the *Apocalypse*, will be appropriate in many circumstances—though clearly not in all, since concealment for self-protection, or protection of others, will sometimes be called for. But we must always remember that the war against Antichrist in the outer world—and even more so the inner world—is also fertile ground for the growth of spiritual pride. What could be more heady than the belief that one is part of an elect remnant called on by God to defy the Beast? We have seen plenty of heartless political and religious fanatics possessed by this idea, and we are destined to see many more. Luckily, triumph in worldly terms is ultimately not possible to the faithful in the latter days, though small victories can still be won. The best we can hope for is that we all— from whatever true and God-given religion we may arise—will some day find ourselves with our backs against the same wall. O fortunate wall! Every hope will be realized there, by those who, through God's grace, have been left with no other hope but Him.

According to some Sufis, Antichrist is precisely the *nafs al-ammara*, the commanding self or 'demanding ego'; the conflict between globalism and tribalism is a reflection of the *apparent* conflict, in the *nafs*, between complacent pride and violent rebelliousness. The following passage is from *Marmuzat-e asadi* of Najmo'd'Din Razi; citations are from the Koran:

Now, in exposition of the truth about Jesus and the Antichrist and the respective contrast and similarity between them, it may be said that the similarity is superficial and the contrast fundamental. From the point of view of appearance they are both called the 'Messiah', and both have a donkey, and they are both alive, and they both bring the dead to life.

Now, Jesus is called the 'Messiah' through traveling the heavens, while the Antichrist is called the 'Messiah' by traveling the earth from east to west. Jesus is heavenly and the Antichrist is earthly. Jesus has vision and confers vision on others; visionary because in his infancy he said, 'Indeed I am the devotee of God' ('Mary', 30), and conferring vision by virtue of healing 'the blind and the leper' ('The Family of Imran', 49; 'The Table Spread', 110), while the Antichrist is blind and a blinder of others, for he presents the Truth as falsehood and falsehood as the Truth. Now, Jesus brings the dead to life as a miracle to provide grounds for faith, while the Antichrist quickens the dead as a demonstration of powers to lure one into denying faith. And the emergence of Antichrist out of the earth serves to bring about a reign of oppression and corruption on earth, while the descent of Jesus from heaven is to bring about a reign of equity and justice.

Be aware that all in the realm of form is a reflection of that which is in the realm of spirit, and all that is in the realms of form and spirit is represented in man.Hence the 'Jesus-ness' in you is your spirit, as of Jesus it is said: 'We breathed of Our Spirit into it [Mary's womb] ('The Banning', 12), while of you it is said: 'I breathed My Spirit into him [Adam] ('Al-Hijr', 29). Jesus brings the dead to life, as the spirit brings life to the lifeless frame. Jesus had a mother, whereas the Divine Breath served in place of a father for him; likewise the spirit (of each person) is mothered by the elements and fathered by the Breath.Jesus is sublime and the spirit is sublime; Jesus is the Word and the spirit is the Word, as indicated by the expression that the 'spirit is by command of my Lord' ('The Night Ascension', 85). Jesus rode a donkey, as the spirit rides the body.

And the Antichrist is represented in you by your 'demanding ego'. The Antichrist is one-eyed, just like your ego, seeing only the world and being blind to the hereafter. Whatever the Antichrist presents as heaven is actually hell, and what he presents as hell is really heaven; by the same token, the ego presents carnal passions and pleasures as paradisical, though they are actually infernal, and it presents one's spiritual devotion and worship as hellish, though they are really heavenly in nature.

The Antichrist mounts a donkey, and your ego possesses bestial qualities. The mystery of it all is that, though Jesus was in the world, as was the Antichrist, Jesus was carried up to heaven for a while, while the Antichrist was locked up in the bowels of the earth. Then, Antichrist will first be brought out to rampage over the earth and create havoc and wreak corruption, claiming divinity. Next, Jesus will be brought down and given dominion, claiming to be the devotee of God. He will succeed in slaying the Antichrist, then set about establishing a reign of prosperity, justice and equity. After a time, he will pass from this world, and the Day of Judgement will be at hand.

In the same way, spirit and ego are brought together in the world of humanity. However, the spirit is taken up into the heaven of the heart, while the Antichrist of the ego is confined in the earth of the human state. It takes several years for humanity to develop its full potential and for the constituents of the body to properly mature. First, the Antichrist of the ego emerges from the confines of infancy, mounted on the ass of animal qualities, launching forth on its program of wreaking havoc in the world, claiming divinity in the manner of 'Have you seen the one who makes desire his god...?' ('Kneeling', 23), and exhorting one toward the hell of greed and lust as the heavenly goal, while decrying the heaven of devotion and worship as hell. He slays the believers of praiseworthy, angelic qualities with the unbelievers' hands of satanic and condemnable qualities, raising the dead powers in human nature, until, all of a sudden, the grace unimaginable bears from on high the Jesus of spirituality, mounted on the regal wings of the Gabriel of the Law, taking flight from the lofty heaven of the heart to descend into the world of humanity.

Reason, left behind, gazes as his departing stirrup,
While Love surges ahead, mounted by his side.

Jesus slays the Antichrist of the ego, by severing his head of material nature, and establishes the dominion of the justice and equity of spirituality in the world of humanity, destroying the swine of greed, shattering the cross of fleshly nature, and slashing the bonds of passion.[2]

When the Antichrist rises, Christ is near. When the ego comes into plain view, the spiritual Intellect, since it sees the whole system of it, is no longer veiled by it; the Eye of the Heart is open. When what we thought was a solid object is seen to be a shadow, then, like all shadows, it bears witness to the Light.

2. *Jesus in the Eyes of the Sufis*, Dr Javad Nurbakhsh, pp 61–64.

Evil, like everything else, is here to teach us. In the beginning it teaches us its own massive reality as a wall which separates us from God, a power to be combatted without quarter. In the end, it teaches us its own emptiness, its fundamental unreality. But until we know its reality, we can never know its emptiness. Until we know that the struggle against evil is entirely up to us, and that the battle will never end, we will never know that, in reality, the struggle against it is God's business alone, and the battle is ended already. It was never necessary. It never began. When, as is predicted in the Hindu scriptures for the end of the cycle, 'a hundred suns arise at once in the sky,' no nothingness can be located; no shadow appears. When God Himself takes the field of battle, He encounters no resistance: because only God is.

We must begin the war against the passional soul, whether seen on the world stage or recognized within, in a state of holy seriousness, fully cognizant of the formidable nature of the evil to be combatted, which initially seems to cover all things. But how can we know evil *as* evil, if evil is all there is? What are we comparing it to in order to make that judgement? What and where is the Light by which we can say 'this is light, and this is darkness?' To ask this question is the first stage of the journey from self-involved illusion to Divine Reality. This journey can be mapped in 7 stages:

(1) We accept conditions with our ego, by identification. Evil is not real, or is at most identified with my experience of suffering, which is a meaningless misfortune to be avoided, even if I must become unreal to do so—as if unreality were a kind of security rather than a name for hell.

(2) Evil is real and external, though basically material. It is not simply my suffering, but the suffering of others too. We must combat it.

(3) Evil is real, internal, and psychological. It is an expression of the 'herd instinct', the mass subjectivity which controls our feelings, thoughts, and actions by means of the 'collective unconscious'. It is combatted through a psychological understanding of our beliefs and motivations, leading to a de-identi-

fication with the unconscious mores collective of society, Jung's process of 'individuation'.

(4) Evil is real, external, and spiritual. We must witness against it in order not to be seduced by it, but we can't overcome it; only God's representative on the field of history, only the Messiah, can defeat the Antichrist.

(5) Evil is real, spiritual, and transpersonal. It is a product of conscious spiritual entities in rebellion against God. It is combatted through the spiritual power of prayer and exorcism.

(6) Evil is real, internal, spiritual, and a concern of myself alone; it is the activity of the commanding self. It is overcome through the act of forgetting self and remembering God.

(7) Since all the evil of the world is merely my own, it is ultimately unreal. Only God is real; there is no god but God, no reality but the Reality. The Buddha sees only Buddhas. What on lower levels we must still call evil is revealed as necessary to God's manifestation, an expression of His Majesty and His Justice.

But the fact that all events are ultimately acts of God, Who is the Sovereign Good, does not absolve us of personal moral responsibility; we have no right to say 'God made me do it.' 'There needs be evil,' said Jesus, 'but woe to those through whom evil comes.' Nor should taking personal moral responsibility be used as a pretext to deny the reality of demonic influence, any more than we should use our recognition of such influence to conceal the ways in which we are affected by the emotions and belief-systems of collective society. Our concentration on these emotions and belief-systems should not blind us to the apocalyptic events in the world around us, nor should the recognition of apocalyptic signs prevent us from doing what little we can in concrete terms when the opportunity for service arises.

Each higher level of our understanding of evil does not negate those below it, but embraces them. The higher level is the true 'informing context' of the lower, which reveals both its necessary limitations, and its precise role in the scheme of things. Therefore the ultimate context, even for concrete service and political action, is the understanding that all events are acts of God; the 'liturgical' way of action in light of this knowledge is simply to play one's role as God has assigned it, assuming He has also given us the light required to recognize it.

THE ESOTERIC APOCALYPSE

When consciousness is centered on the plane of the psyche, experiences arising on the material plane are interpreted according to whether they support or threaten our sense of identity, which is psychic. When consciousness begins to be withdrawn from the psychic plane to the plane of Spirit— which, as pure Witness and pure Knowledge, necessarily transcends experience—then all experiences, including sense experiences, are understood as emanating from the psychic level, and known, simultaneously, both as possible temptations and as actual manifestations of God. Insofar as these

experiences have the potential of seducing consciousness into a re-identification with the psychic level, thus reinforcing the sense of a limited, subjective experiencer, they are temptations. Insofar as these temptations are resisted, the events in question can no longer be called experiences, but are revealed as aspects, or instances, of the Self-manifestation of the Absolute.

On the psychic level, the world we experience is necessarily interpreted in terms of good and evil. And since consciousness fixed on the psychic level cannot witness that level, the contents of the psyche must appear in 'projected' form as the events of our lives. (For all his metaphysical errors, Carl Jung knew this, teaching that 'whatever is repressed is necessarily projected.') But when consciousness begins its pilgrimage from the level of psyche to the level of Spirit, the psyche emerges from that unconsciousness; it is unveiled before the face of the Spiritual Witness. And when, by virtue of that Witness, all events, including material events, are known as emanating from the psychic plane—just as the psychic plane as a whole is known as a dramatization of those *truths* which reside eternally on the Spiritual plane—then the psychic projections upon the material plane are withdrawn. The world ceases to be an object experienced by an individual subject, and is transformed into a visionary apparition contemplated by the Divine Witness— or, in Buddhist terms, by no one.

As consciousness continues to move from psyche to Spirit, events begin to be seen not as good or evil influences, but as forces which either in fact do, or in fact do not, pull our consciousness to identify them, causing it to abandon the Spiritual level and return to the psychic. This is what Sufis mean when they say that 'the sin of the believer is concupiscence; the sin of the gnostic is heedlessness.' Events apparently good can tempt to heedlessness, just as events apparently evil can support mindfulness and spiritual vigilance.

In terms of intellectual warfare, of the struggle to overcome error and embrace Truth, the shift from psyche to Spirit causes the errors we recognize, in ourselves or others, to manifest themselves directly. As we begin to witness them instead of simply criticizing them or struggling against them, they appear before us; they are concretely embodied and fully enacted. In other words, they become lessons— if, that is, we resist the temptation to identify with them—and an error that is really a lesson is no longer a form of falsehood, but a form of Truth. When error is fully embodied as Truth through our own actions, the result is deep and spontaneous remorse. When error is fully embodied as Truth through the actions of others, the result is deep and spontaneous gratitude.

The motion of consciousness from psyche to Spirit, during which latent errors arise, fully-formed and fully-enacted, until they are revealed as forms of Truth, is the esoteric significance of apocalypse, which means 'revelation'. Physical death is a *symbol* of the death of the ego—of the belief that the human psyche is autonomous and self-created. The end of the world is a *symbol* of the 'recollection' produced by the death of the ego—the gathering together of the scattered fragments of the psyche through withdrawal of the projections of that psyche into the abstract wilderness of matter, energy, space and time.

Experience is inseparable from the sense that someone exists who is capable of having experiences. At the ultimate end of the cycle of manifestation, which is the world—at the ultimate end of the cycle of experience, which is the ego—this 'someone' is confronted by

Kali, the Black One. She is *Maya*, she is Mahashakti—at once both the unknowable Divine Essence, and every veil that simultaneously hides and reveals this Essence, with absolutely no distinction between them. To the degree that we try to hold on to our life in the face of *Kali*, she takes that life. To the degree that we let go of our life in the face of *Kali*, she *is* that life.

Experience is *Maya*, it is *Shakti*. If we identify with it, it becomes part of *Avidya-maya*, of the stream of God's cosmic manifestation, the ultimate end of which is 'the death of God'. If we break identification with it, it becomes part of *Vidya-maya*, of the stream of God's redeeming and re-integrating mercy, the ultimate end of which is final Liberation from the bonds of contingent existence.

THE APOCALYPTIC
FUNCTION OF ANTICHRIST

Antichrist is the great scapegoat, who extracts from the soul all that is subhuman, abortive and exhausted, leaving the human substance purely receptive to the light of God. He is not the compassionate scapegoat as Christ is, who bears our impurities willingly, thereby demonstrating that even our deepest flight from God actually takes place *in* God, if we only knew it. As foreshadowed in the figure of Judas, he is nothing but the vehicle which transports all that has failed to attain integral form into the fires of annihilation, because it has refused to submit to God's will, refused to be fully *created* by Him, and has therefore never known Him. And here is perhaps the deepest counterfeit the Antichrist is capable of: to portray the sullen, meaningless, barren suffering of the ego unwilling to let go of itself as the self-sacrificial suffering of that divine Love which 'bears all things, believes all things, hopes all things, endures all things.' In the face of Antichrist, his fascination and his horror, his despair and his blindness, and his unutterable boredom, all one need do is choose the Real and reject what never could be real: simply, at whatever cost, like Christ when he overcame Satan in the desert, like the Buddha when he withstood Mara the Tempter, under the tree of Enlightenment, on the adamantine spot.

The Tibetan Buddhists say: 'roll all blames into one.' In the process, the crimes of a cruel and mysterious fate become the fruits of karma, the consequences of the deliberate actions of sentient beings. The karma of all sentient beings becomes my own karma, the structure of my ego. And finally the crimes and sufferings of my ego become the inevitable shape of THE ego, void of all substance in the face of the Absolute. All are forgiven because no one is to blame but him—and 'he' is no one.

The esoteric meaning of the Antichrist is: that there is only one ego. My ego is THE ego; the God Who dwells in my Heart is THE God. When my ego is annihilated, all ego is annihilated, because there is no other ego. When the God in my Heart is unveiled, He is unveiled for everyone, for all beings, because there is only one Heart. When a saint cries out, 'I am the worst of sinners!' the inner meaning is: I am the ONLY sinner. I am Adam eating the forbidden fruit; by the same token, I am Christ suffering the consequences of this act, triumphing over them, and rising up out of the ruins of them. I am the Buddha gaining enlightenment for himself, and thereby for all sentient beings, because in the eyes of the enlightened Buddha there are no such things as 'numberless sentient beings to be enlightened' nor 'the Buddha who vows to enlighten them.' Enlightenment is One. God is One. There is no god but God.

When I first saw the Antichrist, my response was: 'This means that I no longer have a single enemy on this earth. May all beings be well; may all beings be happy.' When Antichrist lived with me in my own house, he perverted my view of God's universe, he whispered accusations against this person or that person, this group or that group; he claimed they were followers of the Antichrist. But when he left my house to go out into the world and spread devastation, when I saw him rising like a shadow over all the earth, not a shred of hatred was left in my heart. He had nothing more to teach me, except his own emptiness, his shadow-nature. By revealing himself as pure shadow he bore witness to the Light, the great penetrating, searching, unveiling, unmanifesting, and healing light of God now breaking over the world. The breaking of that Light is eternal. It is at the core of every moment. The end of the world lies hidden in every moment. The termination of the cycle, the dissolution of all things, the passing away of heaven and earth, the dawning of the new heaven and the new earth, is always there, in time present pregnant with time future, where the whole creation groans to be delivered— until *now*. 'When a man rejects error and embraces truth,' said William Blake, 'a final Judgement passes upon that man.'

The proper use, the specific spiritual practice of apocalyptic times is: To let everything be taken away from us, except the Truth. When Blake cried, 'Whatever can be destroyed must be destroyed!' this is what he meant. Whoever can—with the aid of Heaven—not reverse, but simply *resist* the tremendous centrifugal, scattering, attenuating and sinking forces active at the end of the Aeon, will find that all the dross in his soul, all the sin, all the spiritual heaviness and intellectual darkness of the latter days, has been stolen from him by the Antichrist. He is welcome to it. By a radical catharsis analogous to the one attempted by the Greek playwrights, enacted not on the Athenian but the world stage, and that of the human soul, Almighty God, through the agency of Antichrist—if, that is, we recognize that Deceiver and inwardly resist him—will literally scare the hell out of us. He will burn out sorrow with sorrow and fear with fear, since only in the presence of God's Mercy can we face the full depth of the sorrow and fear all of us feel at the end of the cycle, and witness their essential emptiness. If we can resist despair in all its forms, including violent panic, cold-heartedness, and false luciferian hope, then, after all the karmic residues of the entire cycle have been torn away from us, there we will stand, naked, in utter simplicity, before the face of God. This is the meaning of 'for the sake of the elect those days shall be shortened,' and 'the meek shall inherit the earth.' Whatever in us 'crystallizes', to use one of Schuon's favorite terms, in the presence of Absolute Truth, will be 'gathered into the barns' where the fertile potentials, the 'seed corn' for the next Aeon, are stored. 'He that shall endure to the end, the same shall be saved': he shall be *saved up*. Whatever withstands the end of time stands at the beginning of time. Whatever is beyond time withstands its end. If 'time is the moving image of eternity,' then that in us which remains untouched by time is part of That of which the image is made. The 'New Age' believes that certain 'highly evolved' human beings can survive on earth to become the spiritual and even temporal leaders of the next

Golden Age; but this is merely the literalistic counterfeit of the true doctrine. The truth is simply that whatever in us resists the temptation to flee from God by taking refuge in chaotic dissolution—to hide from the destruction of matter, or the fear of this destruction, in matter itself, which is one meaning of 'they shall pray for the mountains to fall and cover them'— but dies instead a vigilant and obedient death before the face of the One Reality, will enter the feast of the Pirs, the Shaikhs, the Tzaddiks, the deified Ancestors who are the fathers and prototypes of all cycles of manifestation, they who are called in the book of *Apocalypse* 'the twenty-four Elders before the Throne of the Lamb.' As it *was* in the end. As it *is* in the beginning.

THE PRACTICE
OF APOCALYPSE

In my humble opinion, the central spiritual 'gesture' for apocalyptic times is the following:

When you find yourself in a state of fear or grief over the evil of the world, the degeneration of humanity and the ruin of the earth, know that this evil, ruin and degeneration are nothing but the mass resistance of the world to the impending advent of the Mahdi, the Tenth Avatar, the Messiah—and that the fear or grief you are presently experiencing are *your way of participating in that resistance.* Knowing this, simply stop resisting Him, and let the Messiah come. Stop trying to maintain the world in existence by the power of your ego; let it go. Let it end. Let your ego end. You've been fighting off the Messiah: cease hostilities now, 'resist not evil' (which is how your ego experiences Him), lay down your weapons, and let Him break through 'the clouds of heaven', the clouds of individual and collective egotism which have separated earth from its divine Source ever since the fall of man.

I asked my spiritual advisor to comment on the above paragraph, since advising an unknown public on questions of spiritual practice is not something I have either the right or the capacity to do on my own slim authority. His response was, 'Remember, though: the world is perfect.'

In other words: the Messiah is already here. He has always been here. In each spiritual moment, the world comes fresh from the hand of the Creator. As God is perfect, so His expression is perfect—if, that is, we can witness it, with all its wonders and horrors, as His immediate manifestation. This is the real *Revelation*: 'Behold, I make all things new' (Rev. 21:5). May God, through the grace of my Master, grant me the capacity, and the humility, to know this not only with the mind, but with the whole Heart.

I will end this book, as is appropriate, with the words of Frithjof Schuon:

> Even believers themselves are for the most part too indifferent to feel concretely that God is not only 'above' us, in 'Heaven', but also 'ahead' of us, at the end of the world, or even simply at the end of our own lives; that we are drawn through life by an inexorable force and that at the end of the course God awaits us; that the world will be submerged and swallowed up one day by an unimaginable irruption of the purely miraculous—unimaginable because surpassing all human experience and standards of measurement. Man cannot possibly draw on his past to bear witness to anything of the kind, any more than a may-fly can expatiate on the alternation of the seasons; the rising of the sun can in no way enter into the habitual sensations of a creature born at midnight whose life will last but a day; the sudden appearance of the orb of the sun, unforeseeable by reference to any analogous phenomenon that had occurred during the long hours of darkness, would seem like an unheard of apocalyptic prodigy. And it is thus that God will come. There will be nothing but this one advent, this one presence, and by it the world of experiences will be shattered.[3]

---

3. *Light on the Ancient Worlds*, p 49.